No, I Tell a Lie, It Was the Tuesday

No, I Tell a Lie,
It Was the Tuesday

A trudge through the life and times
of
Alan Maclean

KYLE CATHIE LIMITED

First published in Great Britain in 1997 by
Kyle Cathie Limited
20 Vauxhall Bridge Road
London SW1V 2SA

ISBN 1 85626 248 0

A Cataloguing in Publication record for this book is available from the British Library.

Typeset by SX Composing DTP, Rayleigh, Essex
Printed in Great Britain by WBC Book Manufacturers Limited, Bridgend

To my wife Robin and our son Ben,
and in memory of his elder brother Dan

Contents

Author's Note

The title of this book has been with me for many years and I've remained stubbornly faithful to it. It was my contribution to a casual conversation at an editorial meeting in the 1970s about suitable titles for outstandingly boring autobiographies. I resolved then to use it if I was ever foolish enough to attempt to write such a book myself. So I take this opportunity to explain its origin and to apologise for any irritation caused.

I started to write the various 'pieces' which now make up the whole soon after my retirement from Macmillan in 1984. As the pieces were intended to be self-sufficient I wasn't bothered by chronology or any great urge to get on with the 'next chapter', so there were several happy, guilt-free years in which I wrote nothing at all.

Tess Sacco, an old friend and former colleague at Macmillan, has from the beginning read and criticised the drafts of each chapter as I finished them. Things became less carefree in 1993 when she suggested that I should show my work-in-progress to Kyle Cathie (another friend and former colleague) who had recently set up her own publishing company. This resulted in a contract with an elastic delivery date and a formal commitment to make a book out of the pieces, many of them still unwritten. Now four years later the deed is done. I am deeply indebted to Tess for her skilful and encouraging editing and the patience and good humour that went with it.

I am also very grateful to Frank Tuohy, William Abrahams, Robin Baird-Smith, Robin Denniston, Anthony Flood, George Hardinge, Deborah Rogers, Ann Langford Dent, Jane Sweeney and Ben Maclean for helpful criticism and advice at various stages of the writing.

Especially I give thanks to Anthony and Sally Sampson, who seized on the later chapters one by one and supplied the enthusiasm for and confidence in the growing pile of typescript which I often lacked.

Finally I thank my wife Robin who read everything first and has, among other critical gifts, an eagle eye for facetious asides and no taste for the laborious retelling of irrelevant old jokes. I trust her judgement implicitly and have followed it every time – except for the title, which is where we came in.

ALAN MACLEAN
February 1997

1. *Wonderful Future*

I had an inauspicious start in life when our family doctor confidently diagnosed me as a malignant growth. He told my father first who was suitably horrified and then broke the bad news to my mother who, although 44, had no doubt at all that she was pregnant. She'd already had four children, knew what it felt like and never let him forget it. He had waxed moustaches whose spikes he twitched before pronouncing on any of our minor ailments, knowing, poor brute, that whatever he said my mother would enquire politely whether he was 'quite sure'.

I thought that being a child was a hellish sort of arrangement – three parts frustrating to one part frightening. Mine was by no means an unhappy childhood, I just longed for it to be over so that I could get on with having a good time as a grown-up. This dissatisfaction with my lot was no doubt caused by being by far the youngest in a brood of five (I was 16 years younger than my oldest brother) and although I sometimes heard my siblings complaining, they seemed to have marvellous free-wheeling lives compared with mine. I envied them deeply. In fact they were all good to me in their different ways and did their best to see that I wasn't spoiled too obnoxiously rotten. To be included in any of my sister's games with her friends (she was the nearest to me in age but six years is quite a gap and I bored them to bits) was blissful but my bloody bedtime always came too soon for me if not for them. Almost any involvement with my three brothers was a treat and I particularly envied them their freedom to wear what they liked. I remember, when I was about five, enraging my second brother Andy, then aged 19, by waking him up early one morning and asking him what he was going to wear that day. 'No idea,' he said. I suggested helpfully that he could wear his plus-fours. 'I don't know what I'm going to wear and it's none of your business anyway.'

'But you could wear your plus-fours if you wanted to, couldn't you?'

'Go away.'

I was philosophical about that rebuff but it confirmed my feeling that they just didn't know how lucky they were. Many years later Andy told me that I didn't know how lucky I was to have had our father as a doting old parent instead of a middle-aged martinet. He added, with the closest I ever heard him get to bitterness, that I was also dead lucky that Father had died before I'd had a chance to disappoint him.

My father was a kind and good man but his political world was remote from mine and I don't think that I returned in anything like equal measure the affection which by all accounts he had for me. Perhaps I thought of him more as a rival for the love of my mother than as a loving father and an interesting person in his own right. When someone asked me a few years ago what he was like I said unhesitatingly that I hadn't really known him and that I'd died when he was eight. I realised then that my feelings for him were even more ambiguous than I'd suspected.

He was known to be friendly and even-tempered, a Presbyterian and a solicitor, a Liberal MP for Bath, Peebles and North Cornwall and a lifelong teetotaller. He was Chairman of Ways and Means and Deputy Speaker of the House of Commons throughout the First War and ended up as President of the Board of Education and one of the few Liberal Cabinet Ministers in Ramsay Macdonald's coalition government in 1931. He had many friends and admirers in the House of Commons but my three older brothers, born between 1908 and 1913, found him and his principles a bit daunting. His passionate belief that you should do what you thought was right at all costs was part of their upbringing, but Donald was the only one of us to take it to heart. He was also the only one who was, like his father, a genuine political animal. The cost in his case was high.

My sister was born in 1918 and had, she says, a great time being everybody's darling until, much to our parents' surprise and to her consternation, I arrived six years later. My father was then 60.

My mother was no politician, but she loyally did her best to be a help and rather enjoyed the give-and-take excitements on the hustings. She liked a good fight and, coached and briefed by my father, could hold her own in most situations at election times. She was beautiful as a young woman and blessed with good bones so that she carried good looks into her old age. She used to say that her finest political hour was at one of the annual conferences when she was voted as having the best ankles in the

Liberal Party. She also delighted in minor speech-making disasters and her favourite remembered moment in my father's career was when he was making a rousing patriotic speech at a rally in 1917. 'And where,' he thundered, 'where is the British Navy today? Why, skulking in the Kiel Canal!' She was devoted to this anecdote and I can remember on one occasion asking her where my father was only to be told that he was 'probably skulking in the Kiel Canal'. But she was quite happy being a Liberal and stuck to voting that way for the 30 years by which she survived him. Even in her old age, when the misdeeds of Burgess and Maclean were daily brightening up the breakfast tables of the nation, she continued to refer to Lloyd George (who had split the party beyond repair after the First World War) as 'that traitor' without batting an eyelid.

My three brothers were in their teens by the time I became fully conscious of them and they zoomed in and out of my life at irregular

Bude, North Cornwall, 1925: l. to r. Mother with self, Donald, Andy, Ian, Nancy, Father.

intervals. They quarrelled and rough-housed in a traditional fraternal way but they were friends in spite of the five-year spread in their ages and their quite different temperaments and characters. I enjoyed them most when they were together and they made occasional forays to the nursery on the top floor to borrow my favourite possession. This was an ingenious racing game called Escalado in which six weighted metal horses actually moved along a taut plastic track. By turning a small crank handle the track was made to vibrate and the horses to advance. There were little round wooden obstacles glued to the surface which made the race exciting right up to the line. It had been a Christmas present from a free-thinking aunt and I played it endlessly by myself. But when the brothers came up to play my whole world lit up. They took two horses each, a penny a runner, winner take all. Real money and real gambling and I was allowed to watch but not to take part. I was also sworn to secrecy because our father would not have been pleased. I was flattered by my inclusion in the ranks of the ungodly.

My father had never managed to persuade my brothers to take a serious interest in the history of the clan to which we belonged and they wore their Scottish ancestry lightly. As small boys they had been made to wear the kilt but they regarded themselves as Londoners and the whole clan business as a joke. Their favourite bit of the joke was the clan war-cry and they sometimes amused themselves by hiding in the dark recesses of the house and pouncing on each other (and occasionally on me if I was lucky), shouting 'Another for Hector!' and then running like hell. Ian, the eldest and inventor of this excellent game, explained to me that it was simply the putting into practice of the old saw:

'He who fights and runs away
Lives to fight another day.'

If I had any sense, he said, I'd bear it in mind.

My brothers all went to Gresham's School in Norfolk which was run on an 'honour' system which Donald described to me as an open invitation to betray one's friends. It was there that he and his friend James Klugman (Cluggers to us) first read Marx and became Communists. Although they took it very seriously nobody else did and I believe that Mr Eccles, the Headmaster, and my father were rather pleased that these two clever boys were already responsible enough to take their own political line. They would grow out of it and no doubt be a credit to all concerned. They didn't.

Ian and Donald were successful schoolboys but my middle brother, Andy, had a hard row to hoe. Sandwiched between his two clever and athletic siblings he was plagued by ill health which made conventional school games a torture and he had no taste or aptitude for lessons. He was devoted to Ian, his elder by only fifteen months, but he could never keep up with him. Donald, nearly three years younger and by far the brightest of the brood, was already poised to overtake him in school work when pneumonia set Andy back still further. Our father took the humane option and conceded that Andy had had as much education as he could bear. On the day the other two went back to school, Ian for his last term, Andy bought himself a pipe and had the exquisite pleasure of seeing them off on the school train, puffing on his pipe and blowing smoke at friend and foe alike, all of them for this glorious moment 'boring little schoolboys'. His brothers rather reluctantly saved him from being lynched and he returned to the house well-pleased with himself, airily telling his mother and Nancy that he'd 'put' them on the train. He wasn't equipped to win many battles in his youth so he made the most of the victories that came his way.

Andy had got a job as a shipping clerk at the P & O London office in the Strand but they wouldn't take him on strength until his 17th birthday six months later. Sir Henry Lunn, a friend of my father's, generously offered him the opportunity of going on one of Lunn's world cruises as a supernumerary, junior, assistant purser at a nominal wage. Our parents thought the sea voyage would be good for his health and broaden his outlook. It was also an unspoken recognition that he had put up with many illnesses, several operations and disagreeable years of unsuccessful school life without complaint. In fact he never complained about his real misfortunes but made up for his feats of stoic endurance by maddening both friends and family in small insidious ways. He made himself a master of the craftily disguised insult and he was a genius at evading questions without actually refusing to answer them. He said, no doubt truthfully, that he'd learned the art at school and so his fees hadn't been entirely wasted.

When he returned at Christmas from his round-the-world trip he had a field day evading the many questions about the wonders which he could hardly have avoided seeing. Our mother, exasperated and determined to get something out of him, said, 'Well, you sent us a postcard from Cairo with a picture of the Pyramids on it. What did you think of them?' 'Oh, they were all right,' he admitted, but added triumphantly that Egyptian food was absolutely foul. She consoled herself with the thought that he looked well and that he might well have had a nice time. He certainly wouldn't have told her if he'd had a nasty one. He had a streak of eccentricity and, together with a slight stammer used to good effect, he could turn a boring experience into an interesting if sometimes irritating enigma.

He brought off one of his greatest coups when he was only six or seven years old, accompanying my mother and his brothers on a tedious visit to the local shops near Paddington. Andy tended to wander off on his own and she suddenly realised that he was missing. She wasn't too worried until Ian breathlessly informed her that he was lying in the gutter outside the fishmonger's shop. Ian thought he was unconscious, possibly dead, and she ran back to the motionless figure around which a small crowd was beginning to collect. Afterwards my mother was annoyed with herself for repeatedly saying, 'Andy, are you all right?' partly because he appeared to be unconscious and could not be expected to hear the question but also because she played straight into his hands and she ought to have known better. Anyway he opened his eyes, said he was perfectly all right thank you and closed them again. Her dismay turned to curiosity and she asked him why he was lying in the gutter with his eyes shut. He opened his eyes again and said in a dignified voice that he was just waiting to see if Mr Gow, the fishmonger, would come out of his shop and pick him up.

About 50 years later when Andy was on a visit to London from New Zealand where he now lived, he and I happened to be walking past the shop which still bore the legend in gold lettering JOHN GOW: FISH & POULTRY. I made him show me exactly where he had been lying. He pointed to the spot and I asked him if it had been a highly successful tease or if he'd really been waiting for Mr Gow to pick him up. 'Of course I was,' he said indignantly, 'and in a way I suppose I'm still waiting.'

When Andy was demobilised from the Army in 1946 I was amazed to find that he had invested his gratuity and some of his savings in a new set of tails and a new set of golf clubs. It seemed to me that this was another statement of eccentric preference and I had the sense to accept it with silent respect. Perhaps, like God in the hymn, they were a help in ages past and represented a hope for years to come.

My father had bought a large cottage in the village of Penn in Buckinghamshire. It was on a hillside lane at the top of which a beacon had once been sited and the lane petered out at that point. On a clear day you could see across uninterrupted country to Windsor from the beacon field, which was also famous to us for its annual crops of cowslips and blackberries. There was no electricity until the mid-1930s, but it was big enough for all of us and could sleep nine. My parents loved it and spent as many weekends there as they could, accompanied by as many of their available children as possible. Nancy and I were always available and were sometimes dispatched there for a week or two with a minder. There was an acre of ill-kempt garden, an orchard and a Heath Robinson arrangement for getting shot of bath water by means of a hand pump. Everyone staying there was required to do a minimum of a hundred pumps a day and the smell was terrible. The drains were alleged to have their own subterranean system for soaking away into a small field which had once been the tennis court of a rather smart house not far away. My brothers, who had to do most of the pumping, were convinced that the drains and the bathwater had a secret underground meeting place. They never managed to produce any convincing evidence, but I believed them. Ian used to tell strangers that he was a law student but that his younger brothers were apprentices in the family sewage disposal business. Penn is in Quaker country and people used to write texts in large letters in white paint on convenient blank walls. GOD FIRST was a favourite and Ian got himself into trouble with his father for explaining to one of his Presbyterian friends that it was the result of the local bicycle race. Small beer by today's standards, but in the 1920s blasphemy buttered no parsnips in the Liberal Party.

It was at Penn that my father had the time to catch up with his children and he did his best to get to know me. I wish now that I'd responded more willingly and cheerfully. He quite often asked me to go with him on his favourite walk to a farm at the other end of the village where we fed rotten apples to the pigs. I liked the pig bit but it was two or three miles there and back and he didn't know, or had forgotten, the best way of talking to small children and I could never think of anything interesting to say to him. However, the invitation to the walk was really a royal command

and, after one unsuccessful attempt to get out of it by saying that I was 'rather busy', I used to accept with as good a grace as I could muster. He wore a flat-topped tweed cap and carried a walking stick as well as the bag of apples and he always said 'Good day' to anyone we passed in the lanes. I, an urban child, found this meeting business embarrassing and was unconvinced by his truthful explanation that exchanging 'good days' with passers-by was one of the nice things about living in the country.

I know, of course, what he looked like from the many photographs which I still have but I'm puzzled by the fact that I can't recall his face at all distinctly in any context except one.

I can remember exactly what he looked like on the morning he died in March 1932. His eyes were blue, his face was red and he'd had snow white hair since he was a young man (my mother said that he was a skin short). I went into his bedroom to say good morning and goodbye on my way downstairs to go to school and found him propped up in bed gingerly eating spoonfuls of thin grey porridge. The light from the window was behind him but from the white of the pillows which supported his head and shoulders I could see that his face was porridge-coloured, not red. He looked awful.

'I'm told I must eat this,' he said. 'It'll make me better.' He didn't sound as if he believed it and he looked hard at me across the porridge-laden spoon. A uniformed nurse was hovering about and I got the message that I need not accept the too-obvious lie. Nothing was going to make him better. He believed in the truth and I was suddenly proud to realise that however obliquely, he was treating me as an equal. I felt close to knowing him for the first and last time. I said I would come and see him when I got back from school. He didn't answer but I turned as I opened the door and he smiled and waved his spoon.

The house, a tall, dark, five-storeyed affair on the wrong side of the Park, had been oppressively silent for nearly a week. I'd been in the hall (which was my place for hanging about) when he'd returned in the afternoon in a taxi from his office at the Board of Education, supported by a concerned-looking person. The front door was opened to them as they lurched up to the marble steps and my father's black silk top-hat was slightly askew. I got out of the way and his companion and my mother somehow got him up two flights of stairs and disappeared into their bedroom.

Only a few months before I'd been in the hall at about seven o'clock in the morning when Ian, resplendent in white tie and tails, came in through the front door, shutting it very carefully. When he saw me he put a finger to his lips and winked. His top-hat was at a marvellously rakish angle as he tip-toed up the stairs, a glamorous figure returning to the half-light of a teetotal fold. The party was over and the inevitable row began an hour or two later.

And now the party was also over for my father. Visiting doctors and resident nurses became importantly solemn figures on the scene and it was almost a relief to have to go to school. St Mary's Bayswater wasn't much loved by Nancy, then 13, or by me but it was as good as a pantomime compared with our house in those few days. My brothers were suspiciously civil to each other and to us; our mother, when she wasn't at our father's bed-side, was kept busy answering the telephone and fending off visitors. I couldn't bring myself to ask her or anyone else if he was going to die. I felt sure he was and there was nothing to do except wait for it to happen.

When I got back from school that day Ian was waiting for me. He said nothing but one look at the grave expression on his normally cheerful face was enough. It had happened. We started the long, silent climb up the stairs to the nursery and as we passed our parents' bedroom door he put a finger to his lips, said, 'Dad's very ill,' and we tiptoed on. I don't know how poor Ian had planned to break the news to me but clearly he'd got stuck because he sat silently on the edge of the bath as I washed my hands. I decided to help him out by asking exactly what a heart attack was. He said, 'I'm afraid Dad's gone to heaven,' and I could then decently and thankfully burst into tears. Behind my sobs I was glad it was over, glad of our unspoken conversation that morning. But there, lurking darkly in my mind, spoiling these good thoughts, was a nagging, frivolous, unaskable question – did he have time to finish his porridge before dying?

Ian's turn to die came eleven years later when the converted bomber in which he was the navigator was shot down over Denmark. I still think of him and my father making their separate entrances through that front door – their top-hats on the tilt, the hushed tiptoeing up the stairs – and of my first introduction to irony through one of Jack Hulbert's songs of the 1930s, one verse of which goes:

We've got a wonderful future
One that's rosy and red
You've got me walking on the tips of my toes
And my hat's on the side of my head.

2. *Where The Bee Sucks*

In the summer after the funeral Andy was taken ill again and this time, after much sucking of expensive Harley Street teeth, he was told that he must have a major operation. He seemed remarkably cheerful when I was taken to see him in hospital and said that he was fed up with being ill and that 'kill or cure' was a much better bet. I'd made up my mind that he was doomed but after a month or two he began, to his amazement, to feel well, a state he was quite unused to. He had been off work for a long time and although the P & O hadn't sacked him they weren't actually paying him either and he moved to the London office of the New Zealand Shipping Company where, after a year's trial, he was offered a job in Wellington. It was his chance to get away from his family and have a life of his own and he jumped at it. It fitted in with the break-up of the context of all our lives.

The lease on our large gloomy house was nearly up and Ian, who had passed his final law exams, was heading for a bachelor pad in Chelsea and a partnership in our late father's small firm of solicitors in Lincoln's Inn Fields. Donald, I was told, had become disenchanted with the Reds at Cambridge. He would take the Foreign Office exam when he'd got his degree and it was goodbye to Marx and Moscow. Nancy and I were going to boarding schools, the fees provided by our bachelor uncle, and my mother had her eye on a small house in Kensington, an area which she grew to love and which she was never to leave. So, as Andy joyfully packed his bags, the rest of us were about to do the same – for my part considerably less joyfully.

At the beginning of her Kensington life my mother wasn't sure that she was going to like living there. Paddington wasn't smart but the street we'd been living in had an independent air and she suspected Kensington of gentility. She was quite sure that it was a haven for the old and infirm. But in middle-class terms rents were low and the small house in her sights had a garden at the back and there were white-flowering cherry trees planted in the pavements along both sides of the street. Reluctantly she let furnished the cottage at Penn for three pounds a week. As she also had the income from my father's modest estate and her three older sons were nearly self-supporting she found herself, in her early 50s, with enough money if she was careful and, for the first time since her marriage, with plenty of time to use as she liked.

She loved selling things and, in spite of 25 years of opening and attending fund-raising bazaars of all kinds, she had seldom been allowed to get on the business side of the counter, where she privately felt she belonged. Commerce was what she yearned for and she didn't give tuppence for the view held and expressed by her Cardiff in-laws that to become a small shopkeeper was to dishonour the memory of her distinguished husband. It was true that he'd had large obituaries and that she'd had a telegram of sympathy from the King – 'shan't get another one until I'm a hundred' – and also that her own grief was real and bitter. But none of that was a good reason for public moping and she had no intention of withdrawing from life and, in particular, from the lives of her children, her relations and her friends. She liked to keep an inquisitive finger in as many pies as possible and to have plenty of irons in the fire. She also had a taste for stirring the pot.

The shop was to become her principal iron in the fire for several years and inevitably it played a major part in our lives. After prowling round the shops in High Street Kensington and Church Street she came to the conclusion that what the old ladies would be likely to go for were hand-knitted jumpers, cardigans, twin-sets and woollies of all kinds at reasonable prices. She consulted several friends who were expert knitters and who could do with some extra cash and got an encouraging response. She had no money to invest in stock so her knitting partners had to provide their wares on the basis of 'sale or return' but they seemed to be quite happy to accept the gamble and were harried into recruiting other knitters of their acquaintance.

She found a small grubby shop with a back room in Church Walk, a light and hospitable-looking alleyway which runs behind St Mary Abbott's church from Holland Street down to High Street Kensington. Ian and Donald and some friends undertook the scrubbing, cleaning and painting over the weekend, a new gas fire took the edge off the damp and it looked cheerful and business-like in a few days. She called it The Bee and commissioned one of her nieces, whose mother was related to Burne-Jones, to paint her a shop sign of a pre-Raphaelite bee and this swung proudly above the entrance on the opening day.

Her knitters produced over 60 garments for the opening and The Bee's first customers all came from the remorseless pressure which she put on family, friends and members of the Women's Liberal Party committees on which she had served for so long. The Bee got off to a wonderful start; she sold nearly all her original stock in the first few weeks and her hand-written cards saying 'If you don't see exactly what you want we'll knit it for you' provoked a daunting number of orders.

Inevitably she had to hire a temporary assistant and a telephone and the overheads began to mount. Both Ian and her solicitor told her that her success was going to land her on the rocks unless income could meet expenses and even after a couple of months the overdraft was still going up. My mother responded by advertising in *The Lady* for a hatter and by buying 100 (wooden) jigsaw puzzles to start The Bee Jigsaw Library. Both moves were lucky. There was only one reply to the advertisement and that came from a young woman, Betty McKee, who was clearly a gift from the gods. She not only wanted the job but was so enchanted by my mother and the whole ramshackle enterprise that she offered to mind the shop as well. So Betty set up her hat-making in the back room where she was joined by the 100 jigsaws encased in their hard cardboard boxes. She made marvellous hats which were immediately successful; the customers loved her and so did my mother. She smoked what would now be regarded as a lethal number of cigarettes a day, but my mother had herself taken up smoking cheap Turkish Abdulla No. 1's and she said it made a nice mix. I wasn't meant to smoke, being 11 or 12 at the time, but Betty taught me the art of blowing smoke rings and I had lessons from her whenever I was in the shop and my mother out of sight. I've never forgotten her husky smoker's laugh, her great good humour and her dazzling chic. I asked her occasionally if she was thinking of getting married because although I didn't really expect her to wait for me to grow up I wanted her to remain single for as long as possible. She told me that her one great fear in life was that she would fall in love with a man called Smith and have to choose between losing her true-love and being Mrs Smith for the rest of her life. I didn't think that this problem, dramatic and terrible though it was, improved my long-term chances. When she left 18 months later to get married she told my mother that she'd had a narrow squeak and that she was going to be Mrs Jones.

The shop next door was a tobacconist's and sweetshop owned by a sardonic old man whom I didn't much like. But like most people he took a great shine to Betty and made heavy jokes about her being a down-trodden worker bee slaving away for the benefit of the Queen Bee (my mother) and her young drones (Nancy and me) who demanded royal jelly for their tea. The jokes wore a bit thin but my mother got stuck with the nick-name of Queen and an assortment of her younger friends, including some of mine, called her that until she died.

After Betty's departure I thought that a lot of the fun of The Bee had gone with her, particularly because her successor, Miss Savage, was quite the reverse. Solemn, thin, a non-smoker, 60ish with pince-nez and a bun, she hardly ever smiled. When I complained that Miss S was a poor substitute for Betty my mother said that she was an excellent all-round hatter, an interesting woman, very game and that her straw hats were dreams come true.

No longer shackled to my father's constituency in North Cornwall for her summer holidays, my mother had reverted to Aldeburgh where her own parents had taken their brood of ten in the last years of the nineteenth century until the outbreak of the Great War in 1914. My grandmother, recently widowed at 80, also had good memories of Aldeburgh and had taken to going there for the month of August accompanied by my Aunt Buddie, a tall, sharp, funny and affectionate woman a few years younger than my mother. Buddie had chosen to be the child who remained unmarried to be the mainstay of her parents' lives and who also kept in touch with her siblings and all their various children. Aldeburgh became the annual meeting ground for most of the Devitt grandchildren and my grandmother took up her station on the stony beach in her wheelchair at about 11 every fine morning when she dispensed halfpenny currant buns to her friends, daughters and those grandchildren who could prove by wet hair and bodies that they had braved the cold grey and sometimes overwhelming waves of the North Sea. Buddie was in charge of the buns and was also the intelligence centre for what her relations of all ages were up to.

At that time Aldeburgh was a summer stronghold of the middle classes who rented houses and filled up the four or five hotels from mid-July to early September each year. The bathing was good and the shingle contained a large number of cornelians and, very occasionally, small bits of amber. I was a keen prospector for cornelians and I kept each summer's haul in matchboxes. From time to time one of these matchboxes comes to light when I am looking for something else and I'm transported back to the companionable silence of the daily hunt and the surge of excitement when one found one of these small, transparent stones. I was never old enough to go to the Saturday night 'hop' at the Jubilee Hall, later to be one of the first venues for concerts and recitals when Britten and Pears started the Festival after the war, but this was the high point of the week for my sister Nancy and her contemporaries. It was nice for her that this was at least one game which did not have to include me. Picnics in the heather a few miles away at Snape were nearly wasp-free and occasionally my mother would invite friends with cars and take her party to eat cold bits and sleep out under the stars. I remember lying on my back staring at the night sky thinking of Betty McKee Jones and wishing that Mr Jones had been a resistible Smith.

Two miles to the north of Aldeburgh was the Mere of Thorpeness, a vast shallow, reedy lake dotted with small evil-smelling islands where, for a shilling, you could hire boats of all descriptions for an afternoon's rowing, canoeing, punting or sailing. Children of my age needed no supervision and I used to buy a threepenny packet of five Woodbines for smoke ring practice to add spice to the day's freedom.

In 1937 my mother gave in to the temptation to take The Bee with her for the month of August. She rented the ground floor of a tiny cottage in the High Street and set up shop for a working summer holiday. She was convinced that Miss Savage's straw hats would find takers and she managed to persuade her to join the household. She was quite right; Miss Savage's swooping creations were a hit and, with my grandmother's blessing and Aunt Buddie's enthusiastic help, The Bee had a prosperous month. Nancy and I had had considerable misgivings but the great advantage was that, as a car of some sort was essential to get the stock to Aldeburgh from London and back again, Nancy would be able to put up her L plates and learn to drive. My mother invested in an ancient snub-nosed Morris Cowley which she bought for ten pounds in Notting Hill Gate and which she planned to sell as soon as she got back to London.

I'd learned to be respectful to The Bee's customers in London and to keep my mouth shut unless spoken to. Selling was a serious business and the punters were not to be distracted by childish comments. But the atmosphere in Aldeburgh High Street was much more light-hearted and our friends and relations tended to use the shop as a dumping ground for shopping baskets, wet bathing dresses and such like, which annoyed Miss Savage. However, my mother thought that a bit of extra *va et vient* was good for trade and overruled her protests.

I must have been particularly tiresome in the shop one morning towards the end of our stay because my mother told me that Miss Savage longed to go for a row on the Mere and that I was to take her that afternoon. It was, I think, a penance for me for being annoying and a penance for her for being annoyed. Anyway we took the bus to Thorpeness and embarked in silence on a two-seater rowing boat, I sulking and she apprehensive. I took the oars and she perched in the stern clutching her brown skirt over her bony old knees. It was a lovely day, her pince-nez on her long nose glinted in the sunlight and her plain brown straw hat sat dead straight, secured with a hat pin in her thin bunched hair. She looked uncomfortable and disapproving; I couldn't think how we were going to get through this fiendishly conceived expedition. But quite soon we both began to relax and Miss Savage broke the hostile silence by singing in a pleasant contralto a verse from 'For those in peril on the sea', finishing off with an unmistakeable giggle. I was so surprised that I stopped rowing and laughed out loud. 'Do you believe in God?' she asked. I muttered that I supposed I did and began to pull on the oars again. 'Well I don't,' she said firmly, 'but I always liked that hymn in the days when I did believe in Him, or Her as the case may be.' I'd never come across a grown-up who publicly disbelieved in the Almighty and the idea that He might be a woman was, I thought, wonderful. She told me about her childhood in Liverpool and the nuns at the convent school to which she had been sent. 'I have to tell you that I didn't much care for being a child and I don't now much like children, church or dogs.' She held me spellbound for over an hour but I managed to tell her that I too didn't like being a child, or going to church, but I wished passionately that we had a dog. 'You're not a child,' she said briskly, 'you're a boy and quite soon you'll be a young man and then you can have as many dogs as you like, and you won't have to go to church either. So you've got plenty to look forward to.'

By this time we had crossed the great expanse of the lagoon and were heading back towards the boat-house. She halted the flow of her autobiography and said diffidently, 'Would you mind very much if I had a go at rowing? I've been watching you and I think I could get the hang of it.' We landed at one of the muddy little islands and cautiously changed places. I gave her earnest instructions and pushed us off from the landing stage and for a time she did remarkably well. But inevitably she caught a crab and slid backwards off the bench, her hat still impaled in her hair. She wasn't hurt and although I implored her to let me take over she'd set her mind on rowing us back to base and she did so, pink in the face but triumphant.

As we waited for the bus I had the feeling that I might never have the chance to talk to her again and that she was already retreating behind her chosen façade. I had no words to call her back so I said nothing. As we walked from the bus stop to our house she looked straight ahead as she said, 'Please don't tell your mother or anyone else about my mishap with the oars. I like to be anonymous.' I didn't know what 'anonymous' meant but I guessed more or less right, so I said, 'I'll just tell her that you rowed jolly well.'

I kept my promise (until now) and when my mother asked me how we'd got on I said she'd turned out to be a super oarswoman and that I'd liked her very much. 'I told you she was game,' said my mother smugly.

A few days later we packed up the car with luggage and the remains of The Bee's stock and there was just room for me to squeeze in the back. Miss Savage thankfully took the train.

The thought that the car would have to be sold when we got back made the end of the holiday even worse than usual for Nancy and me but my mother was in high spirits and told us that she planned to sell it en route. 'We don't want to get too fond of it,' she said, and stopped at a second-hand car dealer just off the Bayswater Road. She disappeared into the little office and emerged with the dealer to show off us and the loaded car. 'It's just done a hundred miles with all that on board and it's not even out of breath.'

The dealer was impressed. 'How much do you want for it?'

'Twelve pounds.'

'I'll give you eleven.'

'Done,' she said. 'But you'll have to pick it up tomorrow,' and off we drove.

My mother was ecstatic. 'What did I tell you?' she crowed. 'Where the Bee sucks there suck I!'

I went into the shop on the morning of my return to school to say goodbye to Miss Savage who said that she wouldn't forget our afternoon on the Mere and that she'd try to do better with the oars next time. I asked her if she'd like to come with me to the Oxford and Cambridge Boat Race next year. 'We might pick up a few tips.'

'I've had one tip and I don't need any more, thank you,' she said primly. 'But I hope you get your dog soon.'

Sadly, I never saw her again. My mother said she'd had to retire to look after an old sister in Cumberland. The lease on the shop in Church Walk was up and it seemed sensible to merge The Bee with a large easy-going lady who dealt in antiques and had room to spare (and an assistant to share) up in the busy world of Kensington Church Street. No more hats and I'd lost a friend whom I'd known for one hour and a half.

The small house in Kensington was almost from the beginning too large for us. Nancy and I were away at boarding schools for eight months of the year and Donald was already working in the Foreign Office, having passed the exam in 1935, so he and the Queen had the house to themselves except for school holidays. I think she loved him best of her children and he was very fond of her. He could always make her laugh, gave her good advice, encouraged her to battle on with The Bee and could nearly always calm her down when she was flustered or angry. For me, having him there was a terrific bonus and despite the 11 years difference in our ages our friendship, which lasted intact until he died in Moscow in 1983, began during this time.

There were no Orwellian undertones in our relationship – he was the best sort of big brother to me. Gentle, funny, tolerant and understanding, he always had or made time for me. The only promise he extracted from me was to tell him if my dislike of school life turned into something I couldn't cope with. 'It sometimes looks as if it might,' I said. 'How will I know?' 'You'll know all right, and wherever I am I'll come and get you out.' I treasured that reassurance and, although I never had to cash it in, it made a great difference to my outlook.

I had the run of his large bed-sitting room on the top floor and at weekends when he wasn't working we would often amuse ourselves by singing duets from a songbook of sea shanties and 'traditional' English songs. I got to know (but have now forgotten) all the words to *Over the Sea to Skye*, *What Shall We Do with the Drunken Sailor?*, *The Vicar of Bray*, *Oh No John*, *Drink to Me Only with Thine Eyes*, *Early One Morning* and many more. Sometimes we sang together and sometimes he got out a recorder which he was learning to play and picked out the tune to accompany my wavering treble. Wrong notes didn't bother us and we had no audience to please except for a neighbouring mongrel called Brown who was a regular visitor to our dustbin and would occasionally stay on for one of our private concerts. From time to time we invited Brown to give the dustbins a rest and come for a walk in Kensington Gardens but I never thought his heart was in it and Donald said he only came out of his natural courtesy. I wished I could have called on Brown to help out with my walks with my father at Penn.

Donald was always ready to take me with him if he was going to a movie but he couldn't be doing with the slick American comedies for which I had a great liking, shared by my mother. He really liked what I thought were gloomy foreign films but the Marx Brothers were, ironically, common ground and at one point the three of us trekked up to the Everyman in Hampstead every evening for a week-long revival of their early films.

The fact that he'd given up being a Communist didn't seem to surprise anyone. Our mother, who was ambitious for all of us, told me many years later that she hadn't minded him being a Communist at the time but that it hadn't seemed to her to be very 'useful'. But if he really wanted to go and teach English to Russian children, then so be it. She was delighted by his change of heart and at the prospect of him being a diplomat instead of a Communist. It just hadn't occurred to her that he could be both at the same time.

Communism, I gathered, was something you grew out of, an adolescent complaint like acne. He never talked about it and I don't think I ever gave it a thought. He didn't seem any different to me and, of course, that was the truth of it, he wasn't any different. I told him about the real Miss Savage lurking behind the pursed lips and the pince-nez and he said I was lucky to have been taken backstage as it were and should realise that she'd paid me a compliment. I said that I supposed all those brilliant hats with swooping lines which she'd made for The Bee's customers were the real Miss Savage and that the awful brown straw hat which sat dead straight on her head was really part of a disguise. 'Well,' he said, 'part of being anonymous anyway.'

The lease on the Kensington house came to an end in 1938. Donald moved to a flat of his own and soon afterwards was posted to the Paris embassy. My mother decided to move with the times and into the first of a succession of Kensington flats. Her favourite bus, the No. 52, stopped just outside and The Bee was a penny bus ride away. War in Europe seemed inevitable and in my first term at Stowe we all had to help in the digging of slit trenches in the grounds. Presumably the whole school would rush to cower in the rain and mud when Hitler's bombs came hurtling down on the open Buckinghamshire countryside. After Munich the trenches were filled in and when war finally came a year later the school must have decided that we'd be better off dead in bed and we were spared further digging.

Andy came back from New Zealand looking really well and ready, he said, to do his bit. He let it be known in small slices that he'd been turned down by an unnamed loved one so he was on the broken-hearted list for some time and was also rather cross to find that as yet there was no military bit for him to do. He quickly put the latter frustration to rights by joining the newly invented Auxiliary Fire Service and became a recruit at the Kensington Fire Station. He was a great Gilbert and Sullivan fan and recalled a miraculously apposite aria from *Iolanthe* which goes:

O Captain Shaw
Type of true love keep under
Can thy Brigade with cool cascade
Quench my great love I wonder?

He would sing this to anyone who couldn't escape in time and he also had to explain that Captain Shaw was head of the London Fire Brigade when *Iolanthe* was first performed at the Savoy theatre in 1882. He said it made him feel sad, but definitely better, to keep the torch burning in this simple tuneful way.

It all had a deeply satisfactory ending 14 years later when Andy and his loved one met again in London. His great love had not been quenched and he proposed to her for the second time and was immediately accepted. She had failed to hear him the first time, and it was just his good luck that she had acquired a new hearing aid a few days before this crucial replay.

The last days of The Bee were at hand and my mother arranged a Closing Down Sale which went even better than the Opening Sale four years earlier. Many of her original supporters came and everything went except one enormous mauve cardigan which she decided to keep but could never quite bring herself to wear. 'As good a memorial service as any bee could want,' she said.

We had a last summer holiday at Aldeburgh; it was also the last time the Queen had her whole brood under one roof. Ian brought his wife and baby son and Andy and Donald contrived to get a week's holiday at the same time. I enjoyed myself and them, and my brothers seemed to slip effortlessly back into their easy companionship of the Paddington days, while Nancy, now an attractive 20-year-old, was definitely one of the grown-ups. They all knew, which I didn't, that the Queen was going in to hospital for a mastectomy on 1 September and they combined to let her know, without spelling it out, that she'd done us proud in her first seven years as a merry widow.

On 1 September Nancy and I sat in Aunt Buddie's car outside the hospital waiting for news of how the operation had gone and listening on a portable wireless to news bulletins describing Hitler's invasion of Poland. Two days later the operation was pronounced a success and we were at war with Germany.

I remember thinking that, although I still longed for the day when I became grown-up, the good times which I had blithely assumed went with it might be a bit thin on the ground.

3. *Marching as to War*

I was nearly 15 when war broke out in 1939 and the prospect of going for a soldier was comfortingly distant. I loathed being a schoolboy at Stowe with an intensity which I did my best to conceal. But I made my two oldest and closest friends – the writer Frank Tuohy and the painter, the sadly late James Farmer – there and they didn't seem to mind it so much. I daresay that I'd have managed to make myself as miserable at any other boarding school.

Some years ago my wife persuaded me to take her there because she wanted to see the buildings and gardens and I thought that it might be a good way of laying a few ghosts. It was high summer in term time and everything was looking at its well-worn best. Boys were playing cricket and even the rhododendrons, the trademark, to me, of wet cemeteries, looked good enough round the lake to enhance the beauty of the Palladian bridge and its reflection in the water. But as we continued our tour I found that, far from laying ghosts, I was resurrecting evil glimpses of things long forgotten. The idiosyncratic smells of different classrooms, dormitories, changing rooms, the lake, the library and, for some reason worst of all, the chapel, recreated particular anxieties and dreads which 40 happy years later still retained their power. My wife said that it was difficult to imagine how anyone could live in such a beautiful place and fail to take some comfort from it. I said rather huffily that I could. I wondered how that extremely nice man Christopher Robin Milne, with whom Frank and I had overlapped in the same House for our first year, felt about it.

As time went by it seemed to me that almost anything, including the Army, would be better than Stowe but a windfall in the shape of a closed scholarship to Cambridge meant that I could leave without shame in 1941 and find something more agreeable to do before becoming an undergraduate in the autumn of the next year. It also meant that my call-up would be deferred for eight or nine months and that my mother would not have to borrow more money for school fees. Things were looking up.

I taught for two terms in a prep school which had evacuated itself from Hampshire to Kirkby Lonsdale in Westmoreland. I was paid £33.6.8 a term with 'all found' and I managed quite comfortably on that. The Home Guard took up two evenings a week and although the school staff – all of us being either too old or too young for practically everything – lacked the panache of Evelyn Waugh's prototypes at Llanabba Castle, I used to read bits of *Decline and Fall* to the top form which I had for English and invite them to draw whatever comparisons and conclusions they liked. The Home Guard has been immortalised in *Dad's Army* and that programme's lasting appeal is based on its presentation of endearing human foibles and failings without recourse to caricature. I loved the Kirkby Lonsdale Home Guard and enjoyed it while I could. The real Army would be different.

When I arrived at Cambridge the University was already more than half full of serving soldiers and airmen with a few sailors thrown in who were doing crash courses in scientific, technical and engineering subjects; but some of the Arts courses, including English, History and Modern Languages were still open for business. All the Arts students who were physically fit were required to do two days a week military or RAF training and I chose to follow my brother Andy, who was by that time a 32-year-old recruit in the Royal Tank Regiment; I duly joined the Armoured Corps section. We had to pass a test at the end of the year for a Certificate B, which the War Office had decreed would eliminate the usual months of basic training and fit us for the eight months of officer cadet training, most of it at the ancient Royal Military College at Sandhurst. It was made clear to us that it was as important to get our Cert Bs as to pass our first year academic exams.

On my 18th birthday in November 1942 I was called to the Cambridge Recruiting Office, given my army number (6108149) and a day's pay (3 shillings) and told that I was now a private in the Lincolnshire Regiment. I would not be called up to serve until the end of the academic year in 1943.

I scraped through both exams and celebrated by buying an old bicycle from a friend for ten shillings and riding the 60 miles to London. It took nearly all day because the chain came off every few miles and I took to stopping for a beer and a pee whenever opportunity offered. The Seven

Sisters road must be the longest stretch of public highway without a public lavatory in London and I arrived home with a full bladder and the beginnings of a fair-sized hangover.

With Cambridge behind me there was nothing to do except to wait for my call-up and as the days turned into weeks I started to look for temporary work. When the call came I'd only have two or three days before reporting for duty. I'd heard that there was an agency which supplied 'extras' for the movies so James Farmer, who was also waiting for his call-up, and I presented ourselves at a small dark office off Leicester Square. We were interviewed by Mr Archie Woof, a sardonic old person who told us to check in every morning to see if there was work for the next day. Not many films were being made but we faithfully pitched up day after day to be told 'Nothing today dear'. A friendly old lady who regularly got three or four days' work a week told me I wasn't really Mr Woof's type but that James's prospects were a bit brighter. Sure enough, one day James was called into Archie's inner sanctum and asked if he had a dinner jacket. He hadn't, so Archie said he'd just take James's measurements in case the studio could supply one. James emerged looking rather red in the face and our old lady friend winked horribly and told him he'd have his name up in lights if he played his cards right. Whatever the reason our luck changed for the better and we got two days' work in the next fortnight.

Our first day was a street scene in *They Met in the Dark* with James Mason and Joyce Howard. We were got up as sailors and had to walk past a grand hotel entrance from which the two stars emerged and got into James Mason's car. He said to her, 'Love me, love my car', and she didn't have to say anything. It took from eight in the morning until five in the afternoon with innumerable breaks for cups of horrible tea and cigarettes between takes. We were paid a handsome 25 shillings but thought it a slow sort of business and one could begin to see why film-making is such an expensive affair. Twenty years later when I edited Joyce's first novel I had just taken possession of a brand new Mini – my first company car – which she politely admired. Quick as a flash I said, 'Love me, love my car.' She looked a bit taken aback so I said, 'It's all right you don't have to say anything,' which added to her confusion, and mine.

Halliwell's Film Guide gives *They Met in the Dark* no stars at all and our second film *Yellow Canary* only gets one. But it was a better deal all round for us. An extra five shillings, shorter hours and promotion from

Ordinary Seamen to RAF Squadron Leaders complete with wings, DSOs and DFCs. We looked, we thought, extremely dashing, although another much older extra, dressed up as an admiral, thought otherwise.

'Disgusting!' he said. 'Bloody young shirkers. Ought to be ashamed of yourselves wearing those uniforms and those medals.'

I at once felt more dashed than dashing, but James, rather uncharacteristically, kept our end up.

'Oh yes,' he said, 'and I suppose you're a real bloody admiral, is that it?'

We got on quite well after that and we agreed over cups of tea that as film artistes we had to suffer much for our art.

Yellow Canary starred Anna Neagle and the set was a plywood mock-up of a train and platform at Euston Station. She was an undercover British agent posing as a Nazi sympathiser and was going off on a dangerous mission to infiltrate a spy ring in Canada. Her boss, a full colonel with scarlet tabs and hatband to match, was there to wave goodbye. Anna Neagle was leaning out of her plywood carriage window and to my chagrin James was chosen to look out of the next-door window. As the train began to move the Colonel said, 'Goodbye, Sally, take care of yourself', and the steam was blown up from the ground through a hose-pipe. At the same time the Colonel who was sitting on an orange box on a trolley, was dragged slowly backwards and the shot was ingeniously complete. It appeared to be a Heath Robinson arrangement but it looked brilliantly real in the film. After the first take Miss Neagle reasonably objected to having steam blown into her face. From my place on the boundary of the set, to which I had been relegated to cover up some junk which would have looked out of place on a station platform, I had the consolation of seeing that for the remaining 20-odd takes the steam was redirected to blow into James's face instead. The next day Mr Woof offered us two consecutive days' work for the following week and it seemed that our careers were about to take off. Maddeningly, my call-up papers came through almost at once and on the day that we should have been drinking cups of tea at Ealing, dressed to kill as commando colonels, I was wearing my ill-fitting Home Guard uniform on a slow train to Lincoln.

Lincoln Barracks had an enormous parade ground and that afternoon I sat on my bunk, surrounded by a mass of kit with which I had been issued, and gazed gloomily out of the window across an empty sea of asphalt. I could feel a wave of sluggish panic rising in my gorge and it was almost a relief when we were hustled out on to the parade ground for an hour's drill. After that we were kept on the hop for most of each day and it wasn't really too bad. Haircuts were very short, exposing our thin white necks, and we had to have all our injections in one go, but the dentist parade, which I had been dreading, was a great success with me. I drew an extremely nice man called Captain van der Pantz who stopped about eight of my teeth without hurting me once; I didn't have toothache for another four years. When I did, just after I was demobbed, I searched the London telephone directory in vain for the Captain.

We were at Lincoln for only four weeks and it was during that time that I got a telegram from my mother telling me that my brother Ian was missing. I'd seen him a few weeks before, when the bomber crew in which he was the navigator was on leave. They had just completed a 'tour' (about 30 missions) and were entitled to a spell on the ground, but if they'd opted for that they would have been split up and mustered into other crews when their turn came for another tour of operations. So they'd decided to stick together as a crew and volunteered for special operations which, in their case, meant dropping and sometimes picking up agents in Denmark. They are all buried at Esbjerg. When I saw him I noted the DFC ribbon on his chest and said, 'I see you've changed the rules.'

'What do you mean?'

'The "Another for Hector" rule was that you bashed your opponent and then ran like hell and I don't think you've been doing that.'

'On the contrary that's exactly what we do.'

I still thought that he'd bent the spirit if not the letter of the rule, but he'd loved being an airman and wearing his hat on the side of his head. Terrifying as his death must have been, it had great style and I was proud of him. I wish I'd known him better.

My next stop was Bovington in Dorset at the Armoured Corps Training Regiment where T E Lawrence had been a trooper not so many years before. It was there that he was killed on his motorbike. Our instructors seemed not to be too sure about his standing in the Armoured Corps' pantheon. I recently got to know an old soldier who'd been a recruit at the camp at the same time as Lawrence and asked him what he'd thought about him. 'Not much, really,' he said. 'Couldn't even ride his bike, could he?' *Sic transit gloria mundi.*

The countryside was marvellous and we felt more in the swing of things in our new black berets and being troopers instead of privates. But the regime was strict, petty-minded and humourless. Recruits in training were not meant to have a good time and we didn't. Those of us who'd been skulking at one of the universities for a year had our Certificate Bs and we were in due course sent to a neighbouring War Office Selection Board. There we had to show our powers of leadership and other unspecified officer-like qualities, and also get a clean bill of psychiatric health. It made a nice break from bloody Bovington and only one of the 12 of us was 'Deferred'.

Our casualty was very tall, clever, cheerful and chronically untidy and must have been one of the least war-like soldiers in the world. He and I shared a double-decker bunk and I liked him very much. His trouble was that he was also extremely devout and God featured in too many of his responses to military problems. When it was his turn to show his leadership paces by organising a small group of us over a short assault course, he said very firmly that he wanted us to do it not for him but for God and this was thought to be dangerously eccentric by the examiners. However, he was given another chance later and advised to tone it down a bit. I met him again a few months afterwards at Sandhurst and asked him how he'd managed to make his approach more acceptable. He told me, with his gentle grin, that he'd given it a lot of thought and prayer and that he, or perhaps God, had come up with a solution. He simply prefaced all his shouted orders on the assault course with 'For God's sake . . .' and that seemed to meet the case to everyone's satisfaction.

We were sent to Blackdown in Surrey where we became Officer Cadets and wore white flashes on our shoulders and a white disc behind our mailed-fist cap badge. We were in the same squad as some battle-hardened Canadians who were on their way to commissions in their own armoured regiments, and three charming but very tough Norwegians who had escaped to Scotland and were to be officers in the Free Norwegian Forces. They spoke fluent Glaswegian. They had all been sergeants or sergeant-majors and put up marvellously well with being treated like callow youths. They were very friendly and called us 'the kids'. In return we referred to them as 'the grown-ups'.

Before we left Blackdown for Sandhurst we were told that we could go before yet another board to be trained for armoured cars instead of tanks and I was one of several who applied. Tanks seemed to me to be enormous, noisy, evil-smelling and dangerous affairs, while armoured cars looked altogether more manageable. They went backwards as fast as they went forwards with steering wheels at both ends. They were for reconnaissance and although they went in front of the tanks and infantry they were comparatively lightly armed and their brief was to locate and identify enemy positions and then get out of the way of the heavies who would take them on. The option, if not exactly soft, was infinitely more attractive and I felt that Ian would have approved it as coming within the 'Another for Hector' rules.

At my interview I said the few militarily correct things recommended by others who had been through it – 'Best chance of using one's own initiative with a small fast command, Sir' was the favoured line. In fact there wasn't much else one could say given that none of us had, at that stage, even climbed on to the outside of a tank, let alone an armoured car. So I just hoped that my face would fit. The much-decorated Major giving the interview finally said 'OK, you're in,' and added that there was room for the 'right sort of young officer' in his own regiment. Would that interest me? I could see from where I stood that the Major, who was sitting at a table in front of me, was wearing a pair of marvellous crimson trousers and, although I had no idea what his regiment was, I said without hesitation that there was nothing I'd like better. He wrote my name down in his little book. 'Good,' he said, 'we'll be in touch when you get to Sandhurst.'

I was feeling very cheerful about this but when I discovered that 'my' regiment was the 11th Hussars (sometimes called the Cherry Pickers), who had been among the bravest and best of the Desert Rats, my complacency turned to dread. They were one of the first two cavalry regiments to be mechanised with armoured cars in 1928 and had served continuously in Palestine and the Middle East since 1934. The desert had become home ground to them and they were rightly held to be the kings of it. They had been having a rough time in the mud of the Italian winter and would shortly be back in England preparing for D-Day and the invasion of France. I was heading for all kinds of humiliation in that sort of company and all for the vain sake of those stunning trousers.

At Sandhurst our living conditions were greatly improved. My pay went up from three to five shillings a day and many of the arcane pre-war arrangements of the old Royal Military College were still in place. Ancient civilian batmen still functioned, polishing boots and brasses, blancoing belts and equipment, and the canteen in our building was still called The Fancy Goods Store. We had the great luxury of just two cadets to a room, wore collars and ties and we called our non-commissioned instructors 'Staff' and they called us 'Sir'. I suppose this complicated social charade worked all right though there was never any doubt that the staff had our embryo military careers in their hands. We were neither officers nor gentlemen and nearly all of us understood the realities of the system and knew our place. The six-month course was made up of drill and infantry training, gunnery, driving and maintenance, wireless and finally tactics culminating in a week's trek in the West Country where we practised advancing and retreating in the field. The muddle was certainly realistic.

About half-way through the course I was told to report to the Adjutant one morning. Summonses from this far on high were rare and did not bode well. A friend, Michael Naylor-Leyland, who was in the same squad as I was, had received a similar call and our colleagues were not optimistic about our chances of survival. Neither of us could think of any great sins of commission or omission and I privately put my faith in Michael, who was already an exemplary sort of chap. If he and I were in the same boat then my fate might be not too bad. But those few hours of waiting were tense.

When we got to the Adjutant's office we found two other cadets from one of the tank squadrons and we were quickly told that we were going to a party at Windsor Castle. The King and Queen gave occasional modest dances for Princess Elizabeth and our names (the other three were double-barrelled), the Adjutant said blandly, had come out of a hat. The last lot, he added, had got rather drunk and offered to tip one of the footmen a fiver in the interests of 'cheering up the flunkeys'. Nothing serious, but we would understand that this wasn't quite what was wanted. 'So, don't get drunk.'

I felt a bit like Cinderella although we had to make do with clean shirts, newly pressed battledress, and black shoes and the back of a 15-cwt truck in lieu of ballgowns and a pumpkin coach and four. The dance was quite unlike anything I'd experienced before and my disaster came early before I'd had anything to drink at all. I was trying my luck at an old-fashioned waltz with a nice, pretty girl who was, I think, a secretary at the Palace.

We were doing quite well until I tried to reverse; we collided with another couple. I slipped and down we went like a faller at Becher's Brook. My poor partner hit the floor first and I landed on top of her. We scrambled quickly to our feet and continued at a careful half speed, my partner anxiously looking to see which of her bosses might have observed our crash. If you fall over in a public place everyone thinks you're drunk and, true or false, there's nothing you can do about it. However this was a well-mannered occasion and no one appeared to pay us any attention and the rest of the evening passed happily enough for me and, I hope, for her.

Towards the end I was sitting on my own having a quiet drink when someone came over and took me to the Queen's table and we had what seemed to me to be a wonderfully cosy chat. I thought she was quite lovely and I daresay she thought I was lonely. It made my day and perhaps saved my bacon. The dance finished with a conga and she took me off to join the snake. 'Please, God, don't let me fall over again,' and He didn't. At the stroke of midnight we scuttled off to our truck, like Victorian débutantes, 'our heads pleasurably awhirl'.

D-Day was on 6 June and all leave was cancelled for a few weeks either side of it. Our squad was due for a week's leave and we accepted the fact that we'd had it. But the Commandant ingeniously ruled that we could spend the week within 50 miles of Sandhurst provided that we stayed together as a squad accompanied by, and under the command of, an officer. Our officer was a nice easy-going man and suggested that London was as good an area as any. He knew of a large empty house in Bloomsbury and we could sleep there and use it as a base.

The bombardment of London by flying bombs was in full swing and as we drove up the A30 in our truck one of these doodlebugs overtook us en route for London. We didn't think much about it and as we drove along Kensington High Street I looked idly up Church Street to the block of flats where my mother was living. It was surrounded by fire engines and ambulances and a fair crowd. The truck stopped to let me out. I made myself walk slowly up the street to survey the scene. The front of the building was demolished and the Carmelite Church on the other side of the street was in smoking ruins: but the back of the block, where my mother's flat was, looked to be in better shape. There was, anyway, a fair chance that she wouldn't have been at home to the bomb because I'd tried several times to reach her on the telephone to tell her that I'd be in London and there'd been no answer. I picked my way up the back stairs and found that the front door of her flat was hanging open on one hinge. The flat had three rooms, a minute kitchen and a bathroom from which a low murmur of voices seemed to come. Apart from a lot of broken glass there appeared to be no interior damage but I hesitated at the closed bathroom door. She was quite eccentric in many agreeable ways but I couldn't believe that she was having a bath and a chat while all the rumpus was still going on outside. But I knocked on the door all the same and went in to find her small portable wireless muttering away on the floor by the bath. When I finally tracked her down in a friend's house in Surrey (where luckily she had gone the day before) I told her that the flats had been hit but that hers was more or less OK. I also said that she'd left her wireless on in the bathroom. No she hadn't, she said, but she hoped that I'd had the sense to turn it off.

It was a most enjoyable week and with the help of friends in the squad I got the windows boarded up and the front door mended after a fashion. The fireman's heavy duty axe had made short work of it. I was also allowed on 'compassionate' grounds to spend a night with my mother in Surrey. The wireless business was still rankling and as I left she said quite seriously, 'You are sure you turned the set off? I don't want to have to get new batteries.'

Time passed quickly for us and in August we were told to order our uniforms, so we knew that, barring some last-minute upset, we were all going to get our commissions. I was the only one going to the Eleventh Hussars and my crimson trousers were much envied.

At our passing-out parade we duly slow-marched up the steps in the wake of the Adjutant on his elderly white horse, abandoned our white flashes and dressed for the first time as second lieutenants. It was just over a year since I had sat on my bunk at Lincoln gazing glumly at the great stretch of asphalt with panic rising in my gorge. Now there was just relief and I kept the panic for later.

4. *Another for Hector!*

(War-cry of Clan Maclean)

A week later I reported to Barnard Castle where we were meant to perch until wanted by our various regiments. There I found Ted Pearson, who had passed out a fortnight before me; we were the only two 11th Hussars on the waiting list. He told me that it wasn't worth unpacking as we were off the next day on embarkation leave. I just had time to collect my 'overseas' equipment, most of which was either too cumbersome or too bizarre to be useful. It included a heavy wooden-framed camp-bed, a dear little canvas bucket and an 'Officer's' canvas wash-basin complete with collapsible wooden stand. Ted had already weeded his stuff out and advised me to buy a pair of 'agricultural' (no coupons required) corduroy trousers in which, he said, we would be expected to fight. My mother contributed a sleeping bag by stitching two blankets together and I kept the camp-bed and the bucket. The rest I abandoned at Dover and other transit camps in Belgium and Holland.

The succession of transit camps through which we passed were uniformly dreary, muddy and uncomfortable. They were by nature temporary and tented and the only glimmer of amusement was at the Belgian University town of Louvain where, by kind permission of the mayor, one of the brothels catered for both British Officers and British Other Ranks. A bleary-eyed captain who appeared to be in charge of us said that it was quite 'safe' to go there and, 'Have a bit of fun – do you good, buck you up.'

Some of us felt that, although we should arrive at our regiments as virgin soldiers, we might as well shut our eyes, think of England and hope to establish our manhood, at least in our own eyes.

Trade was brisk that evening and we sat apprehensively in a dimly-lit saloon sipping weak Belgian beer and waiting our turn. Other Ranks had a separate entrance and had to queue. By this time I was regretting the whole plan and was thinking of sneaking off back to camp when the old lady in black who had taken our money at the door tapped me on the shoulder and pointed to the stairs. The result wasn't a complete failure and I thought that if anyone had asked whether I was man or mouse I could claim to be male mouse. When we got back the captain was waiting for us with a broad smirk. 'Have a good time, lads?' and one of my companions spoke the lie for all of us: 'Rather!' he said. 'Topping little grind.'

All too soon, on the morning of my 20th birthday, an 11th Hussars truck arrived for us from somewhere in Holland and Ted and I clambered in, our baggage reduced to kitbag, bedding-roll and our camp-beds. Reluctantly I'd chucked my canvas bucket to which I'd grown quite attached. It was ideal for carrying books, cigarettes and other small items of comfort as we traipsed from one transit camp to the next, but Ted said I'd look silly. 'Might as well arrive with a handbag and gloves,' he said. I took his point.

The regiment turned out to be only 25 miles away and within the hour we were standing nervously in front of the Colonel, Bill Wainman. The week before we'd come across an 11th Hussar subaltern on his way to Brussels for a course and he'd told us that Colonel Bill was a great man. He said that the squadron leaders of B C and D Squadrons were also great men but that he didn't envy us if we were posted to A Squadron.

Colonel Bill didn't waste much time. 'We're here for a few days and there's not much going on,' he said, and a gun went off some miles away as he spoke. I jumped and with some presence of mind slapped the back of my neck and examined the palm of my hand. He looked at me hard but appeared to give me the benefit of the doubt and simply said, 'Pearson, you go to C Squadron and Maclean to A.' As we walked back to the truck Ted said, rather smugly I thought, 'Bad luck you getting A Squadron. But what bit you? We haven't seen a fly for weeks.' 'An ant,' I said coldly, 'so that's first blood to me. Hope you enjoy C Squadron.'

As it turned out I liked A Squadron and its temporary leader, Harry Petch; Ted had the misfortune to find among the C Squadron subalterns one who had teased him unmercifully at Rugby and nicknamed him 'Hearty P'. Ted was once more known as Hearty P until he was demobilised, but he was also well liked and respected, and he and his former tormentor established a wary kind of friendship.

Joining a famous and expert regiment as a newly commissioned second lieutenant in mid-campaign was just as unnerving as I had expected but the 11th Hussars, and others like them, had no intention of entrusting either men or machines to the likes of me until we had served an apprenticeship under the eye of an experienced troop leader. The system was for the new boy to take over the small open-topped armoured car (usually the troop corporal's) known as a 'Dingo'. Each troop had four cars – two large Daimler armoured cars, one Dingo and a White Scout Car containing a corporal and four men who could quickly bale out and act as infantry when needed. After five or six weeks the new boy could expect to be eligible for a troop of his own. However, quite often a troop was commanded by a sergeant and he was always as good as, and often better than, his fellow commissioned troop leaders. There was one such in A Squadron.

I was put in Fourth Troop, where I had a friendly reception. My boss, John Woodhouse, had been a troop leader since 1942 in the desert, Italy, Normandy and Belgium. He'd had many new boys in his time and said, 'You can be as brave as you like but the important thing is common sense.' There wasn't, as the Colonel had said, much going on and I felt a bit less useless and a bit more at home with each passing day. I liked my partner in the Dingo and John Woodhouse and his troop sergeant, Sgt Lovett, a large calm Scotsman with a low voice and a slow smile, made for a confident and contented band. I didn't see much of Harry Petch but he didn't seem to be an ogre. He'd joined the regiment as a trooper before the war and had been a sergeant troop leader in the desert and later commissioned. He had the rare distinction of holding the DCM (when he was a sergeant) and the Military Cross. He'd been second-in-command of the squadron when John Turnbull was wounded in France and had been commanding it ever since. John was due back shortly when Harry would revert to his old job.

My peace was soon shattered by Operation Python which allowed for anyone who had served five years or more overseas to be posted back to England. This caused an immediate vacuum in First Troop, where both the Sergeant Troop Leader and the Troop Sergeant were eligible and their posting home took immediate effect. Sgt Hall had led the troop for two years and the last officer to lead it had been Harry Petch himself in 1941.

I was cleaning our machine-guns one morning and observed Harry and John Woodhouse talking earnestly together. Harry called me over and said with a half smile, 'I want you to take over First Troop tomorrow. I know you've only been here a couple of weeks but both Sgt Hall and Sgt Firth are going home on Python and there's no one else. John thinks you'll be all right and it's a good time to start when we're not busy. Corporal Lewis is being made up to Troop Sergeant so you'll both have to learn as you go along. He's a good man.'

I was so horrified that I couldn't think of anything to say at all. The half smile disappeared and he said sharply, 'Well?'

'Fine. Yes. Good,' I mumbled. He relaxed and said, 'You'll be OK. Just bear in mind they haven't had an officer for a long time. In fact, I think I was the last one. I must go. See you later.'

John told me I'd pick it up in no time and to shout if I needed his help. 'But you won't.' Sgt Lovett came over and said, 'Congratulations. Record time.' I said, 'Thanks but . . .' 'Don't worry,' he said 'You'll be OK. Chance to make a name for yourself.' I thought, 'Yes – "ignorant coward."'

That evening I took my stuff over the to village school where First Troop was billeted. Jack Lewis met me with his new sergeant's stripes on his arm. He grinned and said, 'Look a bit new, don't they?' I said, 'Not as bad as this,' touching the solitary pip on my shoulder. 'We're a right pair then,' he said.

We were soon joined by Corporal Ogden, who had command of the White Scout Car section, and Gary Smith, the new Troop Corporal. We sat in the schoolroom smoking and chatting. All three of them wore the ribbon of the Africa Star and Corporal Ogden also had the Military Medal. We were of course sizing each other up and, although it wasn't exactly a deputation, I felt that they wanted to tell me something. I hoped that it wouldn't be too dismaying. In fact they wanted to ask, not tell, me something but it was nearly half an hour before one of them took the plunge.

'There is one thing we'd very much like to know, and hope you won't mind us asking.'

'Try me.'

'Well, are you . . . do you, um . . . are you set on getting an MC?'

'No, I'm not.'

Three broad smiles and Jack Lewis said, 'Well, then, we'll all get along fine.'

As I lay in my sleeping bag that night I wondered if I'd started all wrong. It was a fair question but I suspected that if I'd been 'the right sort of young officer' they wouldn't have asked it.

I had arrived just in time for the great lull in hostilities which followed the failure of the attempted Airborne coup at Arnhem. It was a bitterly cold winter and we were holding various parts of the line along the river Maas, sometimes in Belgium but mostly in Holland. Although we were never separated from our armoured cars we were doing an infantry job with foot patrols out, sometimes laying barbed wire round minefields at night, and freezing sentry duties. The Germans were similarly engaged on the other side of the river and very occasionally they would send small patrols across to try to pick up a prisoner. In return we would get the Gunners to shell what we thought were their regular posts.

There were mercifully few opportunities for 'making a name for myself', good or bad, but in these months I got to know all the members of First Troop as we grappled with the unfamiliar tasks of our static patrols. Although we were often moved at short notice the job was roughly the same wherever we went and the White Scout section usually had the disagreeable role of manning the most forward listening posts close to the river. One of these was in a ruined house about 200 yards in front of the cars and the farmhouse which served as Troop HQ. The Sappers had laid a minefield just in front of the farmhouse and we had strung great rolls of barbed wire around and beyond it so at least we were protected from blowing ourselves up on our own mines. Sgt Lewis and I took it in turn each night to accompany the scout section down to the post and to check that the line for the field telephone was in working order. They kept in touch with us at the farmhouse at regular intervals throughout the night.

One night I was carrying the field telephone and as I was getting through a hedge I handed the telephone forward to the man in front. When I'd got through I reached out to take it back but he'd already gone on and I thought no more about it until we reached the post. No telephone. Frantic whispered consultation established that none of the three men in front had taken it from me and the man behind had heard me whisper, 'Got it?' as I put it in someone's hands. I went back to the hole in the hedge but there was no sign of it. Luckily we had a spare set at the farmhouse so I went and got that and took it down to the post. As I crawled through the hole in the hedge, clutching the telephone and with panic rising, I had a vision of a queue of silent Germans waiting for another free hand-out. The Scout section, too, made a fruitless search of the area on their way back at first light.

A small nagging mystery; I like to think that our telephone has a place of honour on some German mantelpiece and that an old ex-serviceman is still boring his grandchildren to tears with his long thrilling account of how he captured it single-handedly from a heavily-armed British patrol at the dead of night.

We were generally in the line for four days at a spell and when we were out of it there was time for football, marvellous hot showers at the pit-head baths of a nearby mine, and even a Squadron dance with the local Dutch who were very hospitable and good to us. Seven days' home leave was started for everyone who had served six months since D-Day and there were also 48-hour jaunts to Paris, Brussels and Antwerp. Occasionally we had RAF fighter pilots to stay for a day or two to see what it was like at the 'front'. We had to invent small alarms and excursions for their amusement and they loved spending a night in the line. At that time the regiment had its own four-gun battery for local use and they were encouraged to lay the guns and pull the string.

There were a few return visits and I was lucky enough to get sent to a Mosquito Squadron at Amiens for two days. They even flew me to an airfield in England for lunch. I rang up my mother who was at first delighted and then highly suspicious. 'I'd much rather know the truth,' she said. 'If you're in England and you can't come to see me you must either be wounded or in disgrace. Which is it?' I spent all my pilot-host's loose change in the call-box trying to reassure her that it was neither and that I would write to her when I got back to the regiment the next day.

'Well, darling, if you're *sure*.'

The telephone call wasn't a great success but the flight was marvellous – breaking through cloud at great speed into the blue yonder was the most exciting experience I can remember. I asked the pilot if he'd become blasé about it. 'No,' he said, 'it's wonderful every time. Never misses.'

We crossed the Rhine by moonlight on 26 March. First Troop had the unenviable job of bringing up the rear to pick up and tow any of the squadron's breakdowns. Sure enough, just 50 yards short of the temporary bridge thrown across by the Sappers earlier in the day, we had to stop and hitch up a White Scout car and its crew. We were moving again in ten minutes or so but it was long enough to separate us completely from the rest of the Squadron as we had been overtaken by slow-moving guns and trucks. Thank God it didn't happen on the bridge itself. German fighter-bombers were strafing the area which added greatly to the noise and confusion, but our own ack-ack guns didn't help their aim and they never hit the bridge.

Wireless silence had been ordered and by the time we were allowed to use the set again we were out of range, so there was nothing for it but to keep going east as fast as the traffic would allow.

As dawn came up the countryside looked amazingly surrealistic. Sixth Airborne had landed there 24 hours earlier and the trees were festooned with parachutes and the ground dotted by crashed gliders and supply containers. The first batches of Airborne walking wounded were making their slow way back towards the Rhine and, as we said good morning to them they seemed only fairly cheerful. While we had been crawling along in the dark it seemed to me that our chances of ever catching up with the Squadron were slim but as the traffic thinned and eventually cleared in the early light a reunion began to look possible. I knew roughly where we ought to be but not where we were. We had opened up the wireless set and sent plaintive call signs into the air like a lamb detached from its mother in a field full of sheep. Finally one of our calls was answered and the voice of John Turnbull asked fairly politely where the hell we were. Without waiting for an answer (much to my relief) he said that the rendezvous had changed and gave me a new map reference. Sgt Lewis and I pored over the map and decided to stick to the road we were on in the hope that we should more or less bump into Squadron HQ. We could now hear all the calls on our network and knew they couldn't be far away. As we were passing a group of Royal Horse Artillery guns a brigadier stepped out on to the road and asked us where we were going. I showed him on the map and he said 'Fine, that'll do me' and hopped up on to the turret of my car. Five minutes later we drew up alongside the Squadron HQ cars and handed over the broken-down White and the not-so-broken-down brigadier. After half an hour's break to brew up tea and make a sandwich we set off on our first patrol on German soil.

This turned out to be a major anticlimactic cock-up. We had made good progress on our route, with none of the opposition which the other troops were reporting, and had reached a small wood and been told to go down a reasonably hard-looking track which ran just inside it. Almost at once I managed to get both my and Sgt Lewis's cars stuck in deep mud and we had to wait several hours before we were towed out. While we waited I was taking a look around on foot and came on a small field in which there were six dead black and white cows. They were on their backs with all four legs pointing stiffly to the heavens and their bellies bizarrely distended. Two marvellous surrealist scenes in one day was quite something but not much of a contribution to the final war effort and an inauspicious start to my part in it.

By this time I was quite at home with the troop but I had had no experience of leading it in its normal role of active reconnaissance. Each evening we, the five troop leaders, were briefed on our individual routes for the next day. We couldn't be told what to expect and our job was simply to find out as we went along. Occasionally we were told to check a particular bridge for mines or some other specific task, but mostly it was a question of going along our given routes until we hit something or something hit us. If we couldn't deal with it ourselves the tanks and/or the infantry who were following behind would take it on and we would be diverted to find a way round the trouble. In these last weeks of the war 'trouble' could mean anything from 88mm anti-tank guns hidden in woods, to individual German infantrymen hidden in ditches who fired their bazookas (hand-held anti-tank weapons) at point-blank range. A direct hit from either source was enough to knock out either an armoured car or a tank and of course its crew. There were also enemy tanks and infantry and manned road-blocks, all of which would be trying to hold the German line of retreat and sometimes to counter-attack.

We had powerful binoculars and could sometimes spot 'trouble' before it opened up on us. Jack Lewis had a very good eye and one morning, when we were leading a troop of tanks, he caught a glimpse of what he thought was an 88mm gun about a mile away up in a wood to our right, covering the long straight stretch of road ahead of us. I had a look and thought he was beyond doubt right. I walked back to have a chat with the already rather impatient troop leader of the tanks. I brought him up to my car and got him to focus his glasses on 'our' 88mm. 'Can't see a damn thing,' he said. I suggested that we try to find a way round it and he could then take it from the rear. This didn't appeal to him and he clearly thought we were imagining things. Eventually he said that if I wasn't going on, he was. I couldn't stop him and we let the tanks through and watched them with extremely mixed feelings. They'd gone about a quarter of a mile down the road, and I was beginning to think that I'd made the sort of shameful mistake I'd had nightmares about, when the 88mm opened up and knocked out the two leading tanks. The rest of them swung off the road in different directions and got back in one piece. It was the only time in my life when I've been very glad and very sorry at the same time.

It could of course work the other way round and several days later I'd halted the troop on the outskirts of a small town round which our route lay. We'd seen infantry running across the road leading into the town a couple of hundred yards ahead. Sgt Lewis and I went forward on foot to get a closer look and came to the conclusion that they didn't amount to much. We were walking back to the cars when a troop from another squadron came up fast and stopped beside me. 'What's the matter?' asked the troop leader whom I'd never met. 'Not much,' I said. 'Looks like a few infantry.' 'Is that all?' he said and he and his troop sailed past us and on through the town, leaving me feeling like Hamlet, 'weary, flat, stale and unprofitable'.

The bazooka men posed no such problems because we hardly ever saw them until we were almost on top of them. They would often work in pairs, one on each side of the road, so that they had a double chance of a hit. Many of them were little more than schoolboys recruited to defend every inch of the Homeland and they were very brave indeed.

A squadron had its fair share of casualties in men and machines and at one moment Third and Fifth Troops were both out of action. My friend Peter Newnham, who was in charge of Fifth Troop, had both his armoured cars knocked out by an anti-tank gun and lost a leg in the process. He and his badly wounded driver were in a ditch for two hours before they were picked up by the SAS, who were also operating in the area, as they tried to crawl back to the rest of the troop. Peter had applied a home-made tourniquet and cut off what remained of his leg with his penknife. First and Fifth Troops had been working together that day and he had taken over my original route when First Troop was diverted elsewhere half an hour before. Luck, good and bad, was a major factor in our daily life.

First Troop's worst day was 8 April. We moved off at first light believing that there was, as planned, another troop ahead of us, thereby giving us a 'free ride' until our two routes diverged a few miles further on. In fact there wasn't and as we were not expecting any sort of trouble we were travelling fast when we ran slap into a strongly held road block. It was still very early in the morning and perhaps they weren't quite ready for us, but Corporal Ogden and his White section got two of their bazooka men and successfully attacked the house from which they came. Meantime my car was right up against the road-block and the machine-guns of both the armoured cars and the Dingo were hard at work. I had two wounded prisoners on the back of my car and we pulled back a bit to sort ourselves out. Corporal Ogden was missing. So two of us went back on foot to see if we could find him. The last his section had seen of him was inside the house which was now ablaze. Smoke made it very difficult to see and our search was halted by machine-gun fire and a few grenades lobbed in our direction, so we gave up and scuttled back to the cars. We were ordered to pull back about half a mile and Squadron HQ sent for the wounded prisoners. It was midday before we were allowed to return and we found Corporal Ogden dead. We dug a shallow grave for him at the roadside, marked it with a rough wooden cross and went glumly on our way. He was a man of few words, a nice dry sense of humour and entirely fearless. We missed him very much.

We had good days as well as bad and the regiment was constantly switched to different parts of the Seventh Armoured Division's advances. Reading the laconic prose of the A Squadron War Diary 50 years after it was written I'm amazed at the amount of ground covered in the slog between the Rhine and the Elbe. Sometimes we worked with tanks, sometimes with infantry but mostly we were out on our own. I found it difficult to form even a hazy idea of what was happening on the broad front but there was no real need to know. The Regiment had taken part in the Charge of the Light Brigade at Balaclava and we, like them, were not called on to reason why. But it was nice to know that our fates were in safer hands than Lord Cardigan's.

In the last week of April it was clear that the war in these parts was nearly over but it was an edgy time for us; Bazooka men and boys were still at it and there were small pockets of resistance as well as columns of German infantry looking for someone to surrender to. First Troop had had a frustrating morning trying to clear up a pocket in what was still decidedly user-unfriendly country and had finally to hand the job over to a company of infantry. We were withdrawn and as we brewed up tea while waiting for our new route we tuned one of our sets to the BBC just in time to hear the news-reader enthusing over '. . .the 11th Hussars roaring down the open road to Hamburg'. Jack Lewis said, 'Three cheers for us.'

Home leave had been started back in November and most of the troop had been home and back again before we crossed the Rhine. My turn came on 30 April and as the squadron drove through Hamburg on 3 May, the day of its surrender, I was getting out of the leave train at Victoria Station to be met by my mother who was, I suspected, relieved to find that I wasn't in bandages or handcuffs.

On VE day itself I went to Cambridge to see Frank Tuohy, taking in an afternoon's wartime racing at Newmarket on the way. My aunt had kindly lent me her Austin 10 and Frank and I joined what must have been a nation-wide pub crawl in and around Cambridge. We finally subsided fairly gently into a ditch just outside Trumpington and although it wasn't much fun for Frank it was a happy full circle for me. It was only six weeks since I had ditched two large armoured cars on my first patrol after the Rhine crossing, and, as I switched off the Austin's engine and peered up at the friendly English hedge above us, I felt that I had really come home. No more for Hector.

5. *Berlin 1945-1947*

When I got back from London I found the Squadron comfortably parked in the small town of Brunsbüttelkoog on the Kiel Canal. I duly reported my whereabouts to my mother and she wrote to say that my father would have been proud to know that I was now skulking for King and Country and she hoped that the British Navy was still there.

By this time the unconditional surrender had taken place on Lüneburg Heath and large formations of the German Wehrmacht were laying down their arms and looking for someone other than the Russians to surrender to. The presence of the Red Army just the other side of the Elbe made this an urgent matter for them. A more immediate danger for German civilians (and a major problem for the Military Government) were the Displaced Persons, the name given to newly liberated slave labourers whom the Nazis had imported from all over Occupied Europe. They were now roaming the area in search of food and revenge. Who was to blame them?

There was plenty of work for us to do, ranging from overseeing the civilian administration, guarding food and ammunition dumps, checking that the prisoners of war were still under the control of their own officers, to trying to feed and police the DPs so that some semblance of law and order could be maintained until the 'professional' Military Government arrived to take over from us. We knew that we would soon be going to Berlin along with the rest of the Seventh Armoured Division (the Desert Rats) and it turned out that we had only a few weeks to get ourselves, and our armoured cars, smartened up for the long drive to the East.

Meanwhile we were busy and cheerful and for most of us it was a glorious relief that our war was over and that the daily trials of nerve and competence were over too. We were still living as a squadron but Berlin would mean the beginning for me of regimental life and I had misgivings about that. Inevitably I should be distanced from my companions in First Troop. We had lived at very close quarters and depended on each other for most of every day for seven months and I knew them better than any one else in A Squadron, let alone in the other four squadrons, most of whom were still total strangers to me. As well as the relief there was a sense of impending loss in that the good things, as well as the bad, which had bound us together would sooner or later slip away beyond recall.

The drive to Berlin took us all day. The regiment travelled in convoy and our speed was strictly limited even though we were on the autobahn for the greater part of the journey. As we passed through the check-point at Helmstedt we entered the Soviet Zone and drove sedately down 150 miles of undamaged motorway with open countryside stretching as far as the eye could see on either side. The autobahn was to be the road-lifeline between the British sector of Berlin and the British zone of Occupied Germany until three years later when the Russians closed all road and rail links between Berlin and the West and the year-long Berlin blockade began. But for now it was all smiles and waves and friendly shouts as we passed clusters of ancient lorries crammed with Soviet troops.

We reached the outskirts of Berlin in late afternoon and a large road-sign, erected a few days before by the advance party, announced that we were now in the British sector of the city. To our surprise there was quite a crowd of smiling Berliners, mostly women, children and old men, to witness our arrival. Miles of ruins and rubble and the fact that food was in desperately short supply apparently counted for little compared with their relief that the occupiers would from now on be British troops who, they believed, would be their protectors rather than oppressors. Two months of undisciplined Soviet occupation meant that they had had their fair share of rape and pillage following months of bombing by night and day.

We had been allocated the Von Seekt Barracks in the suburb of Spandau, a few hundred yards from the large gloomy prison later to be the home of the six major war criminals sentenced to varying terms of imprisonment by the Nuremberg Tribunal in 1946. Hess, the only surviving 'lifer', had the place to himself for several years before his death in 1987. Both sets of buildings were more or less intact and although our advance party had been faced with the Herculean task of clearing up the mess left by the Russians, they had recruited over 300 Spandau housewives and made it at least habitable for our first night. They had made bonfires of a mass of decaying meat and vegetables found in the kitchens and cellars, unblocked drains and waste-pipes, and arranged for the burial elsewhere of three human corpses. The body of a dead cow, marooned on an upstairs landing, was found a new home. Saying goodbye to the generous random scattering of human excrement had been another urgent domestic chore.

The barracks had a large square parade ground as its centre and at each corner there was a 20-foot high mound of rotting potatoes. The removal of these vast evil-smelling legacies from our allies had been beyond the ingenuity and powers of the advance party and its gang of cleaning ladies. In those hot July days of our tenancy the stench was overpowering. Flies ruled the air; mosquitoes came later. Eventually bulldozers appeared, potato graves were dug, filled and topped up with earth, stones and cinders and rolled into oblivion. But four fine miasmas hung about for weeks.

Our Spandau ladies still came in every day 'to oblige' and the whole regiment set to work with spades, brooms and paintbrushes; boots were polished, belts scrubbed and brasses burnished and very soon we were ready for daily doses of drill on the potato square. This included early morning drill for all subalterns. No more slouching about in corduroy trousers, scarves and comfortable shoes; our well-worn brown berets were replaced by conventional peaked caps. Separate messes for officers, sergeants and corporals and a large canteen for Other Ranks were established and supplies of furniture (including beds) arrived daily. The quality of the furniture for the three messes and the canteen was much improved by taking a few lorries to the Japanese Embassy in the Soviet sector and helping ourselves to everything from carpets to cutlery. The Russians had still not declared war on Japan and had left the embassy untouched, so we struck lucky.

Our main job was to patrol the streets of the British Sector 'showing the flag'. The idea was reassurance rather than intimidation and we soon found out that roving deserters from the Red Army were both commonplace and dangerous. Civilians had in those early days neither the means nor the right to protect themselves against the troops of any of the four Occupying Powers. Those we picked up were handed over to the Soviet Military Police to meet God knows what fate. They were all Central Asians who had replaced the front-line soldiers a few days after we arrived. The Russians were paranoid about the dangers of their soldiers becoming politically contaminated by contact with the West and we supposed they thought that their Asiatics would be impervious to capitalist propaganda. However, we were not after their political souls – we just didn't want them fouling up our patch.

As the city settled down under Military Government and the hastily constituted Denazification Courts had cleared large numbers of former civil servants (including police) to man the bureaucracy, the need for our patrols ceased. They had become monotonous to us but were as nothing compared with the daily grind of thousands of middle-aged Berlin women who, in head-scarves and pinafores, had been recruited to salvage bricks from the bombed out ruins in nearly every street in the city centre. These ladies worked in long single lines handing bricks politely from one to another. Their code of good manners demanded, it was said, that each lady should say 'please' as she offered a brick to her neighbour and 'thank you' as she accepted one from her other side. The cumulative sound effect 'Bitte-danke-bitte-danke-bitte-danke . . .' was that of a ghost train rattling across the wasteland. Berliners have always made good jokes in bad times.

Shortly after the patrols were abandoned First Troop was detailed to escort one of the first convoys of mothers and children from our sector to the safety of the British Zone. A hard winter was expected and both food and housing were more plentiful in the Zone than in Berlin. The scheme was called Operation Stork and we printed official-looking passes on pink cardboard in Russian, German and English and each adult carried one. There were about 30 rather battered charabancs, each containing 40 mothers and children so we had over a thousand passengers. We had only 150 miles to do on the autobahn and hoped to average 15 mph, allowing for stoppages and breathers, and we carried all sorts of spares and extra fuel. We had our wirelesses going and also two motorbikes as sheepdogs.

Miraculously we'd covered over 100 miles with only two punctures when we stopped to let the children stretch their legs in the heart of the Soviet Zone. There wasn't a building in sight, just fields and a few woods. After the usual five minutes we walked up and down the convoy telling everyone to get back in the buses when one of the ladies in charge of each charabanc reported three children and a mother missing. No one would admit to having seen them go and the search party returned after half an hour without having sighted them. I left one armoured car and one motorbike and told them to wait for another half-hour before coming on. They caught us up empty-handed and we arrived late, worried and sheepishly disgruntled. The Reception Officer at the camp said sagely that worse things happened at sea. No doubt.

Operation Stork was the last time that First Troop and I worked on our own and we were gradually absorbed into regimental life. This looked to me, in its hierarchical structure, ominously like school but the Officers' Mess proved to be a friendly, irreverent affair and I made many new friends among the subalterns from other squadrons. We were a mixed bunch, all of us holding temporary wartime commissions. A few had already decided to apply for regular commissions but most of us were just wondering what to do when we were demobilised. With the dropping of the atomic bombs on Hiroshima and Nagasaki the war with Japan ended on 14 August and World War II was finally and officially over. The government announced its plan for demobilisation based on age and length of service (mine would be due in the spring/summer of 1947). The Colonel interviewed each officer to find out who might be a candidate for a regular commission and what the rest of us wanted to do in civilian life. The Civil Service would shortly be holding written exams for all branches and departments of the Civil Service, including the Foreign Office, so I filled in a form and hoped for the best.

The 11th Hussars was one of the first cavalry regiments to be mechanised but they never ceased to be potty about horses and it wasn't long before the Von Seeckt stables and indoor riding school were back in use. Horses appeared as if out of thin air and they were as mixed a bunch as the subalterns and the dogs, which ranged from greyhounds to dachshunds. The Colonel let it be known that those officers who didn't ride would no doubt want to take the opportunity to learn. I'd had some riding lessons in Rotten Row when I was a child and although I'd got as far as learning, after a fashion, to rise to the trot I'd found it more frightening than exhilarating. It was the only good thing about being sent away from home to boarding school – no horses. But anxious as ever to please I put my name down and horse life began.

The beginners' class happened every morning in the indoor school at 11 o'clock sharp. I was given a thin, depressed-looking bay mare who had been liberated from a cart. I knew her groom very well because he was also the gunner/wireless operator on Sgt Lewis's car in First Troop and had volunteered for the job. I'd asked him at the time if he was sure that this was what he wanted to do. His face lit up. 'God, yes,' he said, 'I've been with horses all my life. Nothing better.' He was a small Welshman, Taffy Lewis, built for fitting into the cramped turret of an armoured car as well as for riding work on racehorses. He'd already christened the mare Rosemary and he assured me that she was a good thing in the making. 'Half-starved she is. But she's got class and she'll go a bit when we've built her up.' I said I hoped he wouldn't build her up too quickly. I couldn't ride at all. 'You'll learn fast enough and she's a kind horse, you'll see,' said Taffy.

We were taught extremely well by Tommy Pitman, a major recently returned to the Regiment after three years as a prisoner-of-war, who combined his expertise with patience and humour. I gained a brief notoriety early on by suggesting, in answer to a question, that one of the ways of getting a horse to go forwards might be to stub one's cigarette out on its neck. But it earned me a life-long friendship with Jimmy Burridge who sometimes amused himself by joining in the class and who many years later bred and owned the famous grey steeplechaser Desert Orchid. It was after this incident too that Tommy lent me a pair of long leather chaps which, by making me feel like a Red Indian Brave, did wonders for my morale. The other thing which steadied my nerve was a glass of *vieille cure* (a delightful mixture, I think, of Benedictine and brandy) taken at a sly gulp just before the daily school. Anyway, with the help of Tommy's kindly tuition, the loan of the Red Indian outfit and the magic gulp, I kept going from stage to stage without too many disasters and I found myself enjoying horse life. Sometimes we rode three times a day – before breakfast above Spandau on the heath, known as the Old Sewage Farm, school in the morning and back to the Sewage Farm in the afternoon 'for fun' – the dogs came too. All this time Rosemary was improving in health and looks and she proved to be a natural jumper. I knew that her rate of progress already outstripped mine and that she could cart me anytime she liked when we were up on the heath. But she had such good manners that she nearly always pulled up when asked and her behaviour in the school was impeccable. Tommy had decided that when we could all jump down a line of low-slung poles while taking off our battledress tunics without falling off he would stop the course. I was the last one to achieve this and that was our grand finale.

I was due for another week's home leave in October and when I arrived I found my mother packing a suitcase. 'Where are you going?' 'Hospital,' she said briskly. 'I have a lump, classified, I'm told, as a conundrum, so I'm off to the London Hospital in Whitechapel. Sorry to spoil your leave.' It was lucky for all of us that my sister Nancy was working in London and staying at the flat. My mother's conundrum was an enormous abdominal tumour which caused her no pain but the discomfort was already beyond a joke. She'd been growing it for some time and had planned to let it be until I'd had my leave. But much to her annoyance Nancy had spotted it (you could hardly miss it) and called in the doctor.

The London Hospital pulled very long faces and surgeon after surgeon said that because of its size the conundrum was inoperable. My mother was quite well but getting impatient and no one had yet had the courage to tell her that nothing could be done for her. Just as well because the last surgeon on the Hospital's list, a refugee from Central Europe, said that he'd once successfully removed a tumour of similar size and wouldn't mind having a go. By this time I'd already extended my leave twice and had applied for Andy, now a staff sergeant in the Intelligence Corps in Italy, to be given compassionate leave. I'd been told that there was no doubt that he'd get it but we'd had no word from him. When we met the surgeon he gave a great grin and a shrug and said, 'Well, I did it before. Why not again?'

The young registrar was deeply pessimistic. 'A very long shot, I'd say.'

'Maybe,' Nancy snapped, 'but kindly don't say it to her.'

We spent the afternoon before the operation with her and as we were leaving the young registrar came in. We said goodbye and that we'd come and see her the next day when she came round from the anaesthetic. The registrar standing beside me muttered, 'If . . . not when.' I don't think she heard him but we waited for him to follow us out and Nancy said, 'I think you must be insane.' He shook his head and went on his way. Going home on the top of a No.12 bus we didn't say much but I remember asking Nancy if she knew whether people had to be invited to funerals or whether they just came.

The operation, however, was a great success and they said we could come to see her later in the day. I brought some letters and a telegram from some of her cousins sending her loving wishes. She was still quite dopey but her eye caught the orange envelope of the telegram. 'What's that?' she demanded. I read her the message. 'Bloody wishes? Bloody wishes? I don't want their bloody wishes!' and with a beatific smile she went back to sleep. After that short but telling performance we knew she'd be all right. She was very proud when next day she was told that the conundrum was to be bottled and placed in the London Hospital archive. 'Probably their Chamber of Horrors,' she said modestly, 'but a non-malignant horror they tell me.'

Two days later Andy arrived, none too pleased to be home once he knew that all was well. I asked him what took him so long. 'Combination of bloody you and the bloody Army. There's no such thing as compassionate leave from Italy. They offered me a compassionate posting or nothing, so I had no choice really. But trust you to dig me out of a comfortable villa outside Florence and get me dumped in a Military Police barracks, all for nothing.' I could see that it was a bad deal for him but the Army had done its best by posting him to a barracks no more than 200 yards from my mother's flat and he was given immediate compassionate leave from there. When my mother came out of hospital he was allowed to sleep at the flat and potter down the road after breakfast. He was then 36 and his release date only three months away. When I left he said, 'Don't let me keep you from the fleshpots.' I don't think he ever quite forgave me.

We'd known for some time that Colonel Bill would be handing over to Colonel Payne-Gallwey, of whom terrifying tales were told. He was coming back to command his old regiment and majors who had served with him for years said that he was a fire-eater who ate subalterns for breakfast. We wouldn't like it but it would be very good for our souls. The noise of people taking their fingers out would be deafening. Every cliché about retired colonels applied except that this one wasn't retired and was about to make our lives a living hell. At that time there was a famous Russian football team called the Dynamos who were knocking spots off every British team they met on their goodwill tour of the UK. It seemed a pity to us that the new Colonel couldn't be diverted to command the Dynamos instead of us, and he was known as the Dynamo long before he arrived. He'd taken over ten days before I got back.

Within two hours of my return the Dynamo called a meeting of all subalterns and captains as a result of some rumpus at one of the Officers' Clubs the night before. I felt quite relaxed because it couldn't possibly have had anything to do with me and I sat confidently at the end of the front row. His tirade was impressive: 'Haven't come back to command a regiment officered by hooligans', and so on. But the odd thing about it was that although his voice was gritty, his tone incisive and his message venomous, he also appeared to be smiling. I was coolly observing this phenomenon when he paused, looked straight at me and gave me a brilliant smile. I smiled ingratiatingly back. 'And,' he snarled, 'you, whoever you may be, can take that stupid grin off your face!'

I knew that the Dynamo had been a fearless and successful amateur steeplechase jockey before the war but I didn't know that he'd been kicked in the face by flying hooves when he had a fall at Aintree. This had left him with a permanent half smile on one side of his face. If I'd been sitting at the other end of the row I might have missed it. Not a good start for me.

That evening as he looked thoughtfully round the mess he was heard to say that there was a lot of dead wood to be cleared out. Naturally, after that, there wasn't a self-respecting subaltern who would describe himself as other than dead wood.

My dead-wood status was confirmed quite soon. I had a message from Kit Steel, the Foreign Office Minister in charge of the Political Division of the Control Commission in Berlin. Donald had worked for him in London and had written from Washington to say that I was in Spandau so Kit asked me to lunch at his house in the Grünewald. His staff were mostly regular Foreign Office bodies but there were also a few Army officers seconded from their units who shared some of the work. He asked me what I was going to do when I was demobbed so I said that I was going to take the Civil Service exam in the hope of getting into the FO. 'Oh well,' he said, 'you'd better come and work for me. I'll be losing two of my soldiers quite soon. Be good practice for you and if you're even half as good as Donald was at your sort of age you'd be a help to us. Will your colonel let you go?' I said that I didn't think our new colonel would be averse to getting rid of me, but equally I wasn't sure that he'd want to oblige me. Kit told me to ask him. If he said yes then that would speed things up, but a negative wouldn't matter much, it would just take longer.

My interview with the Dynamo was even worse than I'd expected. My loyalty, he said, was to the regiment, not to the furtherance of my civilian ambitions. If the regiment required me to stay I stayed. If it required me to go it would decide when and where. So I was to tell my Foreign Office friend that the answer was no and that was the end of the matter. And by the way he'd been going through the month's mess bills and mine was one of those which made it clear that I drank too much. Halve it by next month, or he'd write to the Foreign Office and tell them that I was an alcoholic in the making.

The mess bill problem was easily solved. Those of us who had been ordered to halve our bills simply charged every other drink to more temperate friends whom we repaid in cash. The sums involved were small because we mostly drank cheap German gin and equally cheap good German hock. So the Dynamo was appeased and none of us went thirsty. As for my being an embryo alcoholic the Dynamo turned out to be quite right, but I suspect that it was a random shot which found its mark.

I went to see Kit again and he told me to wait patiently. The Foreign Office would ask formally for my secondment in London and although it might take a couple of months the request would not be refused. I would, incidentally, be promoted to captain because the Control Commission didn't deal in anything less. He didn't suppose I'd mind that too much. He would still be one soldier short. Did I know of anyone suitable?

As it happened I'd told a new friend, Tony Flood, about my problems and he said he'd like to come too. He'd joined the regiment before D-Day, had been given a Military Cross and had been persuaded by Colonel Bill to apply for a regular commission. The bait was a posting to Australia to work for a general who had been in the regiment in his youth. However, the arrival of the Dynamo had changed things and when the posting came through the Dynamo said he wasn't satisfied that Flood was committed to the regiment and gave the job to someone else. Tony now regarded himself as a piece of dead wood and was keen to try his hand at something else. After an interview with Kit his name was added to mine and nothing was said to the Dynamo.

The Dynamo turned up on the last day of Tommy's beginners' course and had a good look at all the horses. Rosemary was looking a picture and it seemed to me that he was taking an unhealthily long time admiring her. A day or two later he asked me if I knew that she was blind in one eye. When I had to say that I didn't, I realised that our days together were numbered. I asked Taffy Lewis if he'd been turning a blind eye to her blind eye all this time. 'Oh, yes,' he said, 'but she sees fine with the other one and I thought it might put you off if I told you.' Quite.

In fact, the Dynamo delayed his take-over of Rosemary until we had publicly disgraced ourselves in our one and only appearance in a novices' show-jumping event on the airfield at Jever near Wilhelmshaven, where the regiment had been moved in the spring of 1946. It was a hot Saturday afternoon, our event the last on the card and we were number 16 out of 25 entries. We had a long wait which made me even more nervous than usual. There was a beer tent (but no *vieille cure*) and I had some of its wares, which made me sweat. At last our turn came and the sight of the brightly painted poles and the crowd made Rosemary snort and shy. She took the first jump at a gallop, demolished the second, ran out at the third, swerved back on her tracks to take the first jump back-to-front and bolted across the open grass of the airfield. About a mile later I fell off and was rescued by jeep. Rosemary trotted back to join her friends and received a round of applause from the spectators.

That evening the Dynamo cornered me in the mess. 'That mare's come on a lot, Alan.' I still couldn't tell whether he was smiling or snarling but his voice wasn't hostile. 'She's too much for you now so I'm going to take her on and see what I can do for her. You can have my horse if you like.' There! It was done and no bones broken. At least our partnership had ended with a bang, not a whimper, and I had no regrets. The Dynamo was a great deal more sympathetic to horses than to people and Rosemary would be in good hands.

I didn't take up the Colonel's offer of his horse. It had two eyes, both of them mean. Instead I was given a portly old mare and we ambled sedately round the airfield. She didn't care for jumping and I have to say that when Rosemary went most of the fun went with her.

Our posting to the Political Division came through, as if out of the blue, a few weeks later. The Dynamo sent for us and waved the offending documents under our noses. 'If you tell me you don't want to go I can have these orders cancelled.' We stood to attention and said nothing. 'Right. Pack your stuff and get out.' We caught the night train to Berlin and sewed the extra pips on to our battledress jackets on the way.

I didn't ride again for 45 years, when I took up with my present companion, a 25-year-old cob with the build and looks of a dwarf shire-horse and a mind of his own. He likes to jump over small natural obstacles in the woods and I tell him tall stories about my life in the cavalry which he clearly doesn't believe.

In the two months of our absence in Jever nothing except the weather had changed to improve the lot of the Berliners. But even that short time away was enough to make us realise that Berlin had come to life since we had first arrived, in what appeared to be a dead city, to patrol its desolate streets in our armoured cars. The basic food ration was still barely at subsistence level and, although the acres of rubble had been tidied up a bit, finding somewhere to live or even to shelter was still an acute problem. On the other hand daily newspapers, one or two magazines and the wireless were active and now schools, cinemas and even the Opera House were open. Civilians in the streets looked smart if not chic and the search for food had gone underground to the black market, supplied chiefly by the occupiers with cigarettes (the currency in all four sectors of the city) and tinned food. Black market fresh vegetables and meat found their way in from the surrounding Soviet Zone. The ban on 'fraternisation' had been formally lifted and the illegal night clubs were now legal.

A number of undamaged houses and blocks of flats had been taken over for the use of members of the Western Control Commissions but this caused remarkably little resentment. Berliners in the three Western Sectors knew only too well that their position in the middle of the Soviet Zone was precarious and that the presence of British, American and French troops and officials represented their only hope for the immediate future.

The Nuremberg Trial of the 22 major Nazis accused of war crimes (three of these were acquitted on all charges when the trial ended in September 1946) had been going on since November and there was daily coverage in all newspapers and on the wireless. So if I felt a pang of shame as I ate bacon and eggs for breakfast I managed to get the stuff down without too much trouble.

Whatever the pace of change in Berlin itself, the change for Tony and me was immediate. As newly promoted captains we ceased from that moment to have any military duties at all and although we still wore uniform we worked and lived as civilians. Tony was assigned to work in the Chancery where the daily flow of telegrams and correspondence with London kept several third and second secretaries on the hop. He lived in the Political Division Mess which he found agreeable and comfortable. I was slightly disconcerted to find that I was to live in Kit Steel's mess which contained two old friends of his, a retired brigadier who had been Military Attaché at the British Embassy in Berlin before the war and Ralph Thicknesse, a full Colonel in the Ulster Rifles who had served for many years in Palestine. I needn't have worried; they all got on extremely well and went out of their way to make me feel at home. In return for living in great comfort I poured out drinks for Kit's many visitors but otherwise had no domestic responsibilities.

I'd brought my year-old black spaniel, Rupert, with me and I wasn't too sure how he would take to office life, let alone life with the nobs. He was the only survivor of a litter of six who had been struck down with distemper as puppies at a time when there was no antidote available. It had left him with collapsible back legs, but he was an affectionate and sociable dog and he was made welcome. The butler, who had been head waiter at the Adlon Hotel, took a great fancy to him – a fancy which was devotedly reciprocated. Rupert had a day-time basket in the kitchen where snacks and company were available at all hours. His life, like mine, changed immeasurably for the better.

In the autumn the ban on wives for the Control Commission was lifted and the arrival of Kate, Kit's wife, improved things even more. She was short, bespectacled, benign and very funny. She brought with her a small car and their three school-age children were also allowed to come and stay for their holidays. The retired brigadier retired again so the mess became a household with Ralph and me as lodgers.

The only sadness was the presumed death of Rupert. He had the run of the small garden and was last seen ambling about there. If he had somehow climbed the fence and wandered up the short drive to the road he might have been run over. But it was more likely that he had been stolen for food. It's easier to cope with death if you know how it happened and for weeks we half-expected him to re-appear collapsibly apologetic. His butler friend refused to remove the basket from the kitchen but eventually Kate persuaded him that enough was enough.

Kit was tall and straight-backed and this, with his pepper-and-salt moustache, gave him a military air. He liked soldiers and had enjoyed dealing with generals when he was attached to SHAEF (Supreme Headquarters Allied Expeditionary Force) and Berlin was stiff with them. Some of his SHAEF friends were now neighbours and others were commanding this or that in the British Zone and they often came to the house. I got quite used to them and Kate, herself the daughter of a general, thought they were all ducks. When I looked doubtful about this she said, 'You just have to feed them regularly and stand no nonsense.' I privately gave them duck ratings from 0 to 5 but there was only one who earned the dreaded nought in my little black book. He was brought to the house one Saturday by a Grade 5 duck and I was giving them a drink before lunch. He loathed me on sight and wanted to know what on earth I was doing there when I should be putting in useful time with my regiment. 'The Americans would call you a "cooky-pusher",' he said nastily. Kate arrived to hear this attack and waded straight in before I had time to answer. 'Don't be so silly, General,' she said briskly. 'Alan doesn't like his regiment; he likes living here with us. Now come and have some lunch.' There was nothing more to be said and I glanced nervously at the Grade 5 duck who had commanded the Seventh Armoured Division in France and held the 11th Hussars in high esteem. He gave me a wink and with a broad grin said, 'Well, that's sorted that out.' A very nice man, but it was the stuff of which nightmares are made.

Berlin was the seat of military government for the four Occupying Powers. Once a month the Control Council, in the persons of the four Commanders-in-Chief, accompanied by their political advisers and hangers-on, met to rubber-stamp the rare agreements reached by their Deputies in the Co-ordinating Committee or to take note, by way of lengthy prepared statements, of their disagreements. Below and reporting to the Co-ordinating Committee were the various Four-Power directorates which covered the full range (except of course defence) of conventional government departments e.g. finance, economics, transport, education, political, trade etc. They met at least once a month, sometimes once a week, and the chairmanship of all these bodies rotated on a monthly basis.

This cumbersome, multi-layered method of providing a central government for the whole of Occupied Germany was intended to reflect the unanimous will of the four Occupying Powers until such time as it was feasible to agree a peace treaty and to hold elections leading to the formation of a democratic German government. It was, of course, doomed from the start. There was no such thing as unanimity, least of all as to what the word democracy meant. By 1946 the American honeymoon with the Soviet Union was over, the Iron Curtain was in place and the Cold War had begun. The three Western powers set about the business of restoring democratic (our version) political parties and practices in their respective zones and sectors of Berlin. Vast injections of Marshall Aid, allied to currency reform, were givien to kick-start the West German economy. In the meantime the Soviet Union set about replacing the Nazi party with the German Communist Party and drawing up plans for ejecting its three partners from Berlin itself. The Western presence, both political and military, in the heart of what was to become East Germany (the German Democratic Republic) was rapidly becoming intolerable. The Soviet blockade of West Berlin began in 1948 and lasted nearly a year.

Somehow the façade of Four-Power government and all its trappings remained in place. Although propaganda had replaced argument and the meetings, at whatever level, had long since ceased to achieve anything of importance, it suited all four powers to keep in reasonably cordial touch.

I was put to work as assistant to Ronald Scrivener, a Second Secretary, who was amongst other things the British secretary on the Four-Power Political Directorate. Ronald was a good mentor. Fluent in both French and German, he had plenty of 'grasp', that elusive quality much prized by ambitious young diplomats. As far as I could see, it meant being able to analyse problems, to pick out the important bits and having a recognisably responsible view of what might or might not be done about them. The proof of the grasp-pudding lay in the further ability to write all these things down briefly and comprehensibly with not more than one modest joke per page. Those with grasp might become serious high-flyers in the Service.

Although Ronald was clearly a candidate for higher things he was also good-humoured and entertaining and we soon became friends. I had a desk in his office and after a while I found my way through and round the mass of papers engendered by the Political Directorate and could fish out the right ones for our boss before each meeting. Ronald took me with him to agree the minutes produced by the secretary of whichever nation was in the chair, and when it was our turn he encouraged me to do the first draft. So slowly I got the hang of how things worked. It wasn't much of a test for grasp but I was quite hopeful.

Sir William Strang, the Political Adviser, was a slightly built man of some solemnity. He was a Grade One Ambassador, already near the top of the Foreign Office tree, and he had his own private office, which was in theory separate from Kit's Political Division. He used our services which included taking Ronald with him to the meetings of the Co-ordinating Committee and Control Council to draft the telegram which would report the proceedings. Ronald did this impeccably (leaving out the jokes) and was allowed to take me too as part of my education. Sir William moved at great speed and when faced with stairs took them two at a time, his staff panting in his wake. He was known to them, fairly affectionately, as Whizzo. He had the habit, when deep in thought, of putting two fingers to his pursed lips and making a soft tuneless whistling sound through them. Occasionally someone would claim to have recognised a tune and it was said that *God Save The King* was the best sign of a fruitful thought process and *What Shall We Do with the Drunken Sailor?* not so good. Either way underlings were not recommended to interrupt it.

Sir William was impressed by Ronald's grasp and before long took him away to be his Private Secretary. This left me to grapple with the Political Directorate stuff and Tony was moved over to share the load, such as it was. He had by this time fallen in love with our opposite number in the American Political Division and a great deal of consultation went on between them in and out of office hours. Esther was most attractive as well as being a dab hand at getting Mr Plimak, the Soviet secretary, to see things her/our way when it came to agreeing the minutes of each meeting. Tony had his own way of coping with Mr Plimak which involved a regular exchange of bottles of Scotch for caviar wrapped up in old copies of Pravda. Tony and Esther duly married and were 'officially' allowed to live together in Esther's flat for their last few weeks before Tony's demobilisation. The Political Directorate celebrated their nuptials after a meeting by drinking their health in (still) Caucasian champagne.

Since our brilliant careers as film extras had been cut short by our call-ups in 1943, James Farmer and I had only met in London when our leaves briefly coincided. He'd been commissioned in the Rifle Brigade but his spondylitis had grown steadily worse and he was ruled out for active service. His elder brother had a permanently stiff neck and it looked as though James was heading in the same direction. He was stuck at Regimental Headquarters training recruits until the end of the war when he was seconded to Military Government (no training for that) in a pleasant German town near Hanover. I spent a weekend with him there and he told me that he had applied to join the War Graves Commission whose job it was to register the graves of British soldiers and airmen buried in France and the Low Countries and to arrange for the coffins to be returned to the UK if the next of kin so wished. He was duly interviewed, given an oral test in German and was accepted with alacrity. 'Not a job everyone wants to do.'

A month or so later his posting to Berlin came through and he began to smell a rat. He was promoted to Captain and told to report to No. 1 Graves Concentration Unit. His Commanding Officer was an ancient, lugubrious major with a fine line in black coffin humour (I never found out his real name because he was known exclusively as Bones) and he explained the vital difference between Graves Registration and Graves Concentration. 'You're in luck, Jim,' he said. 'This is the real stuff.' True enough. There was to be no driving about rural France with a notebook, lunching with friendly mayors. This was taking a three-ton lorry into the Soviet Zone with a lot of spades and plastic bags for days, sometimes a week, at a time. James was quite philosophical about the twist his military career had taken. He became fond of Bones and his two fellow grave-diggers and their mess was comfortable, though it didn't attract many visitors. He'd brought with him his dog, a beautiful long-haired dachshund bitch called Häschen (little hare) and she took to her new surroundings with grace and enthusiasm. Bones called her Hazy, and Hazy she remained. She accompanied James in the lorry on his expeditions and was, he said, a great help in breaking the ice with the Russian officers and East German officials on whom he depended for directions, food and casual labour. Jokes about bones for the dog were inevitable but she took it all in her ladylike stride.

Hazy also accompanied James when he came to the Steels' house. Although Kit and Kate did their best to put him at his ease it was quite obvious that he felt profoundly uncomfortable. His visits were only made tolerable by Hazy's stunning talent for making friends. She was affectionate and inquisitive but never a bore and when James went on leave to England she was invited to stay. She was already on friendly terms with the butler, took to using Rupert's old basket in the kitchen and slept on my bed.

All went well until, on the fourth day of her visit, she disappeared. No one saw her go and although we searched the neighbourhood we had no real hope of finding her. After the loss of Rupert we could be forgiven for taking the worst for granted.

I wasn't looking forward to breaking the bad news to James and rang up Bones to find out when he was due back. Bones told me and added huffily that he thought I was meant to be looking after the dog. She had turned up there two days earlier, tired and hungry but otherwise well. The Unit was, for obvious reasons, based round an isolated warehouse which meant that she had travelled about ten miles crossing two railway lines and a river on the way. She had never covered any of the ground on foot before. I suppose that in spite of her good manners she found life with us, without James, a poor substitute for home. Bones said that after eating a large supper she went straight upstairs to James's room, jumped up on to the bed and settled down to wait for his return. Bones left the bedroom door open and from then on she came downstairs for meals and a chat and would only go outside for personal reasons. Otherwise she stayed in bed until James got back.

It turned out that James's and Hazy's Berlin days were nearly over. He and I went to a concert at the Opera House one Sunday afternoon and as we were leaving we passed the brigadier (not one of Kate's ducks) in charge of British Troops Berlin. He took exception to James's effort at a salute. His spondylitis was always at its worst when he had been sitting down for any length of time and he was walking in a sort of extended crouch, which made it almost impossible to turn his head in either direction. He'd managed to get his right hand up in the general direction of his cap but the result was more of a dismissive wave than a salute. The brigadier said that he was a disgrace to his uniform and that he'd have him out of Berlin the next day. He was as good, or bad, as his word and Bones and I saw James and Hazy off on the night train to the British Zone and a doubtful future.

Bones had already been on the telephone to his boss in the Zone to explain the reason for James's expulsion and to give a glowing report on his work. 'Don't worry, Jim,' he said. 'The Colonel will see you right and get you a good berth till you're demobbed. You've done well for us and sod the brigadier.' Bones, like the brigadier, was as good as his word and when James rang me up a few days later it was to say that he'd been made a judge (a junior one) on one of the Military War Crimes Tribunals. These were mini-Nuremberg trials, run on court-martial lines with their findings subject to confirmation by the Judge Advocate General's

Department. I wondered what the other British judges were like, but James must have given some satisfaction because they asked him if he would sign on for another year. Some other time perhaps.

Kit's most frequent visitors from London were the historian John Wheeler-Bennett and Pat Dean, then Head of the German Political Department at the Foreign Office. Both had been at Nuremberg, Pat as one of the Foreign Office legal advisers and John attached to the British Prosecuting Team. I liked them very much and they both offered me work when I was demobilised.

John was something of an expert on German affairs and had published two major books before the war, a biography of Hindenburg in 1936 and a massive work on the Treaty of Brest-Litovsk in 1938. He was just finishing a book on Munich. As a sideline to his writing in the 1930s he bred racehorses at a stud near Hanover. He knew many of the Nuremberg defendants and also got to know the old Kaiser whom he continued to visit after the war. He was suspected, rightly no doubt, by the Nazis of being an agent of British Intelligence and after the stud was ransacked and burned down in 1937 he escaped back to England. He and Pat had been commissioned to write an account of the Nuremberg Trials but he was already pessimistic about the chances of Pat getting enough time to do any real work on the book.

On one of his visits John had just read an obituary of Angela Brazil, whose famous novels about girls' schools gave him endless amusement. I suggested that he might write her biography and forget about Nuremberg. 'No,' he said after some thought, 'but if I had the right sort of collaborator I might have a go at becoming her successor. No tongue-in-cheek stuff. Just straight.' We spent an enjoyable evening roughing out a synopsis for *The Beastliest Girl at St Bea's* and he suggested that we should each do a sample chapter. He was of course much too busy and I had no idea of how to set about it, let alone the ability, so the project joined the Nuremberg book on his list of things not yet done. When, seven years later, a benign fate landed me up with a job at Macmillan, his publishers, the first thing he said was, 'Now we can get on with the book.' But his *Life of King George VI* got me off the hook.

Pat's offer of work was much more straightforward. The Four-Power Council of Foreign Ministers was due to meet in London in the autumn and his department was going to need extra hands to staff the British

Secretariat. This meant long hours and low pay but it would be good practice and I would find all subjects up for discussion abysmally familiar. I could have time off to take the Civil Service exam (again) and I could join the department as soon as I liked after demobilisation. I accepted gratefully and the next week I had a note from the Personnel Department confirming my temporary employment for an indefinite period at a salary of £326 a year.

6. *Getting It Right*

Lines on the Formulation of British Foreign Policy

In a high-ceilinged room in the Office
With Gainsboroughs lining the walls
A distinguished old man with a briefcase
Sat thoughtfully scratching his balls.

He might have been thinking of Tito
Or planning a minute on Greece
The results of the German elections
Or how to get Honour and Peace.

He might have been brooding on Stalin
And if it would pay to be frank
His steady grey eyes were as clear as could be
And his mind was an absolute blank.

Like most small boys I found that grown-ups tended to fill conversational gaps by asking me what I wanted to be when I grew up. One of the conventionally acceptable answers for the very young was 'engine-driver' so I used to say that. When I reached the age limit (about six I think) for this being a satisfactorily cute response I was left with a sulky 'Don't know' which irritated my mother. She demanded that I think of something short and sensible, adding that it didn't have to be true or interesting, just suitable. Observing the mulish look on my face she said, 'Why don't you say Member of Parliament like Dad?' So I did that and that was fine. It wasn't true but it was sickeningly suitable and everyone was pleased. It served very well until Mr Harris, the headmaster of St Ronan's, the prep school to which I was sent after my father's death, changed it for me.

Mr Harris was an immensely reassuring figure. Straight as a die, a former Soccer International for England, a Christian gentleman, he was completely at home in prep-school life and mores. Good things were often described as 'ripping' and bad ones as 'mouldy'. I don't recall much chat about the rise of the dictators in the early thirties but there's no doubt that he regarded both Hitler and Mussolini as a bit mouldy and would certainly have said so if asked. His heart was in the right place.

However, I do recall an afternoon in the winter of 1936 when the bell had just been rung for rehearsals for the school play (scenes from *The Tempest* with Lindsay Anderson as Caliban. Mr Harris wrote in the school mag that 'Andy ma is the best Caliban St Ronan's has ever had'). Mr Harris stopped me to say, 'Mac, you'll be going for the Diplomatic, won't you?' I was always on the look-out for his approval and answered quietly and responsibly, 'Yes, sir' and was rewarded by a satisfied nod. It was the first I'd heard of it, but his assumption that this was my chosen career gave substance to the idea and I happily adopted it. Donald seemed to be having a good time there and I was glad to be shot of the future MP tag.

But Mr Harris was no fool and when I left the school in 1938 he told me that he'd thought, when I first arrived, that I might turn out to be one of the best people to pass through his hands. The beginnings of a self-deprecating simper were wiped off my face when he continued, 'Well, you're not. You're much too keen on making yourself popular with all and sundry and not sticking up for what you believe to be right.' So he knew what I was like and I daresay he thought he might instil moral fibre into me by calling me 'Mac'. Men called 'Mac' are, in my experience, likely to be sturdily independent, possessed of worthwhile values and ready to fight for them. Only one other person in the last 70 years has called me that (unless ironically) and she was a very pretty girl to whom I was much attracted. But I knew as soon as she started calling me 'Mac' that we were both on a loser.

Mr Harris and I remained on friendly terms although we seldom met. He must still have thought that my unMac-like qualities would be OK for 'the Diplomatic', although that was hardly flattering to it or to me. Anyhow, he volunteered to be one of my referees when I was a candidate for the post-war Civil Service Reconstruction exam, which was in two parts. The first was a written exam at which point the absolute goats were separated from the possible sheep and politely shown the door. The second was the country house weekend selection board when the best young sheep were drafted into the various ministries, including the Foreign Office. I didn't have to call on Mr Harris for a 'character' because I failed the written part (twice) and was therefore prevented from showing off at the weekend beano. I wondered and still wonder how he would have phrased his reference without scuppering my chances and/or offending my prospective employers.

While this process of recruitment and reconstruction was going on there was room for cheap casual labourers in the Foreign Office and abroad. I later found that my lack of career prospects was a positive advantage for getting odd, interesting things to do.

My first day as a temporary sheep started with a shock. I turned up at the Downing Street entrance at 9 a.m. and negotiated my way, escorted by a dignified Office Keeper in an elegant dark blue frock coat, to Pat Dean's office on the first floor. I was expecting to be put to work in the large room where the Second and Third Secretaries had their desks and telephones. Some of these I knew slightly and I had corresponded with most of them on minor matters during my last year in Berlin. Not too daunting. These people were after all collectively the 'Dear Department' to whom we'd addressed our letters, signing them, 'Yours ever, Chancery' and I no longer found this sort of formality funny or frightening. On the contrary it was comfortable, verging on the cosy, and I was looking forward to the approaching meetings of the Council of Foreign Ministers at Lancaster House. This was to deal only with Germany and the chances of finding anything on which the Russians would be likely to agree with their three Western partners were just about nil. I had been hired to help with the drafting of the minutes, collating briefs for our own nobs and generally being a useful dogsbody.

Pat was on the telephone as I was ushered in but he gave me a friendly wave. 'Yes, all right,' he was saying. 'He's just arrived and I'll send him along in about ten minutes.' He put the receiver down and said 'Look, one of Lord Pakenham's private secretaries is ill and that was the Personnel Department telling me to lend him someone for a week or two until this chap's recovered. The fact is that I can't spare anyone at the moment, so I'm afraid it'll have to be you. It won't be for long and it's all good experience for you. Martin Anderson's a good fellow and he'll look after you, and you know where I am if needed.'

I followed Pat down the corridor and he opened a door and said, 'Martin, this is Alan Maclean to help you out. Hasn't been with us long, but it's the best I can do,' and shot out again.

Martin, who looked rather solemn, said, 'Oh, good. Come in. The Lord won't be in till this afternoon so there's time for me to show you some of the ropes. By the way, how long have you been in the office?'

'Almost exactly a quarter of an hour.'

He looked stricken at first and then began to laugh. 'Tell me something about yourself, and then I'll tell you something about the Lord and we'll see where we go from there.' I told him what I'd been doing and the temporary nature of my job in the German Political Department.

Martin looked mildly encouraged and said that Frank Pakenham's job as Chancellor of the Duchy of Lancaster was a bit of a fudge. He was a junior minister but not in the Cabinet and he minded passionately about what sort of a new Germany we should be aiming for. He had a finger in many pies at the Control Commission, but he wasn't actually responsible for what they did. He had no licence to be involved in anything in the way of foreign policy, which was strictly Mr Bevin's pigeon. You could say that he had a responsibility for helping to formulate British policy towards the German people in our zone of occupation, if that made it clearer. It didn't really so I just nodded wisely. Martin added that Frank was very clever and a very nice man too, as I'd find out, but although he was not averse to publicity he was absent-minded and 'administration' was not his forte. He thought it best not to tell him too much about the length and breadth of my Whitehall experience. Just that I'd been working in Berlin and was now doing a stint in London.

I never found out whether this fine-tuning of my credentials helped in any way because I don't think Frank ever quite realised that I was meant to be working for him. Whenever I took him a batch of telegrams or papers to sign he would thank me profusely: 'It *is* kind of you, thank you so much.' Rather as if he'd fallen off a bus and I, a passer-by, had helped him to his feet and handed him his hat. Once he said to me, 'I must have a long chat with you about these plans for new secondary schools in the Zone.' But mercifully he was much too busy for chats, as his correspondence was large and he attended what seemed like a continuous lava flow of meetings. In the four weeks I was there I got quite good at answering the telephone and drafting replies to innocuous letters but I never discovered what it was that he actually did. We remained a mutual mystery to each other and when I left he said, 'Are you off? Do look in again soon and we'll have that talk.' A few months later Frank was promoted to be Minister of Civil Aviation. The French Ambassador, M. Massigli, observed that it was an excellent appointment and a convenient one, too, in that Lord Pakenham would not now need to descend from the clouds.

I, however, was brought down to earth with a bump when I heard I'd failed the Civil Service written exam for the second time. I assumed, wrongly, that the Personnel Department would be informed of this and would hoof me out, but I decided to sit tight, say nothing and hope for the best.

The Council of Foreign Ministers ground its way through the winter months and if its achievements were non-existent it generated and wasted a colossal amount of paper. Mr Bevin's last meeting with Molotov at the first CFM in Moscow in 1946 had produced one of his classic one-liners. Molotov had accused Mr Bevin, at great length, of protecting Nazi war criminals and persecuting freedom-loving democrats in the British Zone of Occupation. Bevin got fed up after a time and interrupted to say, 'Well I never shook 'ands with 'Itler, more than some can say.' I'd been hoping for more of the same, but no such luck and the excitement of sitting in the same room as these heavyweights soon wore off. Someone told me that Molotov's Russian nickname was Kameni Zad (Stone-bottom); certainly he never appeared to move in his chair and his large, square, bespectacled face gave nothing away. Vishinsky, his deputy, was the reverse. Flamboyant of speech, dress and gesture, he snarled and sneered with a vulpine smile. His reputation was villainous and he looked the part.

The Russians clearly did not intend to be held responsible for the failure of the session and were remorseless in filling the time with long, detailed diatribes against their Western counterparts. It seems likely with hindsight that they were clearing the propaganda decks for their blockade of Berlin early the next year (1948) when they hoped to force the three Western Powers to give up their rights to their sectors of the city. They had to abandon the blockade less than a year later in the face of the successful airlift and the Western embargo on imports from the entire Soviet bloc. The Council of Foreign Ministers never met again and both Molotov and Vishinsky were sacked and humiliated by Khruschev after Stalin's death in 1953.

When this great charade was over I thought that I'd better confess to

Pat that I'd failed the exam again and was therefore due for the boot. 'Oh, bad luck,' he said, but told me to stay put and help tidy up. Something else might easily crop up.

As it happened the News Department was looking for a replacement. It was an 'irregular' department in that nearly all its members were unestablished and I was invited to try my luck.

Rids (William Ridsdale) had been recruited to the News Department in the 1930s and had been head of it for nearly ten years. Small, dapper, quite sharp and often funny, he and his deputy, Norman Nash had been established during the War and were now venerable figures honoured with the Foreign Office decoration, the CMG (Companion of the Order of St Michael and St George). They were respected and trusted by their customers – the Foreign Editors and Diplomatic Correspondents of the British Press and the London Correspondents of foreign newspapers etc – and by the rest of the Foreign Office including successive Foreign Secretaries. The customers liked them because they were not 'career' diplomats and because, as former newspapermen, they were sympathetic to the pressures under which journalists work. Their colleagues in the FO liked them because they kept the Press off their necks and were remarkably skilful at putting over the Government's view on the current issues and crises of the day. The days when this could all be done by two or three people were long gone and, apart from Rids and Norman, there were seven of us working in a heap, each of us specialising in one or more areas or subjects and responsible for keeping in touch with the Departments concerned.

At first sight the News Department appeared to be chaos and I couldn't see how it worked at all. The telephones rang nearly all the time and our visitors were legion, but I soon fell in love with it.

Rids and Norman had their own offices where they held court with their particular customers and dealt with such paperwork as came the department's way. The rest of us milled about in an enormous room, the arena in which the daily Press Conference was held at 12.30. It contained three long tables, lots of chairs and most of our telephones. There was also a small room leading out of the arena which boasted a couple of desks and telephones, a Reuters ticker-tape machine which clattered out hot news and round-ups from all over the world, and a safe for the daily batch of incoming telegrams. One of us came in early to read through them and mark up the interesting bits. There was hardly room enough for us all to be in the room at the same time but we had no need of desks of our own and no paperwork. All our work was done on the telephone or face-to-face and we travelled very light.

The Twelve Thirty was the central point of our day. A short list of 'topics' was made up first thing in the morning after someone had done an early trawl through all the morning newspapers. We could make an educated guess at what would be the main stories on which we might be asked for a reaction. If the Department concerned authorised a formal statement which could be attributed to a Foreign Office spokesman, we all had a copy to keep handy. But the Twelve Thirty was a free-for-all and everything said by the man in the chair was on the record. In my time it was nearly always Peter Matthews, but he could call on any of us to take a particular question so we all had to be ready to speak up if needed.

Peter was the longest-serving of the seven Irregulars and the rest of us recognised him as *Primus inter Pares.* He enjoyed the Twelve Thirty hugely, however hostile the questions. He was there to be shot at but was also at liberty to shoot back, provided that he didn't stray into the grey areas beyond his brief. He was a brilliant performer, dealt good-temperedly with all questions, loaded or otherwise, and his grasp of foreign affairs lent weight to what he had to say, whether on or off the record. He was also severely handicapped. He had lost most of his sight in a childhood accident and had one glass eye and about half the sight in the other. By holding the page very close to his sighted eye he could read well enough, albeit slowly, and he relied on his colleagues to tell him which of the press cuttings and telegrams were worth the effort and time. We also took it in turn to read some of them aloud to him and his memory and ability to identify and assimilate important points hidden in a mass of verbiage were remarkable. He had chronic asthma which killed him in the late 1950s.

Not everyone liked Peter and he and Norman got across each other from time to time. Norman was white-haired, kindly and avuncular and had been the perfect foil for Rids's waspishness in all the years of their partnership. He had time for everyone and correspondents, British or foreign, who had any sort of grievance tended to go to him to have their ruffled feathers smoothed. He would promise to 'have a word' with whichever of us was the object of the complaint and conscientiously did so. Most of us didn't mind this method of keeping the customers (however tiresome) happy but Peter didn't much like being lectured by Norman, or indeed by anyone, and had perfected the quite difficult art of getting him to lose his temper. Peter named these rare eruptions 'foulmoutheries' and would sometimes refer to Norman directly as Lord Foulmouth. He did so at one meeting in Rids's room and Norman leant across to him and said 'I'm an exceptionally nice old man and don't you bloody well forget it.' After years of patient peace-making Norman was rather proud of his Foulmouth title.

The Twelve Thirty attracted 30 or 40 regular customers representing many nationalities and most shades of political persuasion and there was a sense of wary camaraderie among them. The man from TASS, the Soviet News Agency, never missed, made copious notes but never spoke, while the *Daily Worker* kept the Communist end up and could be relied on to try to get some fur to fly. However, on the morning of the day in 1949 when the Grand National was run, someone noticed that the *Daily Worker* had tipped a horse called Russian Hero and Peter politely enquired whether this selection was endorsed by TASS. 'Of course,' he replied with a broad smile, 'unless it is sabotaged by the British Government.' This, his only utterance within living memory, earned him a round of applause. That afternoon Russian Hero won the great race at odds of 66-1 and the following Monday when Peter offered the News Department's congratulations both TASS and the *Worker* got a standing ovation from their colleagues.

Beneath and aside from all this on-the-record business, which was conventionally attributed to 'A Foreign Office Spokesman', our most interesting and even useful task was to provide off-the-record guidance on any subject to any well-disposed journalist who cared to ask for it. We hoped that he would incorporate it in whatever he was writing that day. If he needed to quote a source for off-the-record material the convention was to use 'diplomatic circles', 'usually reliable sources' or 'informed quarters'. We had to get to know all our regular customers, British and foreign, and, much harder, to judge how indiscreet we could dare to be in each case.

Some correspondents chose to form small groups which would meet and talk to one of us at regular intervals, others preferred a daily chat in person or on the telephone. Rids himself had three regular sessions every day. At noon the diplomatic correspondents of the *Manchester Guardian*, Reuters, the *Daily Herald*, the BBC and the *News Chronicle* would gather in a privileged huddle in his room for a briefing on whatever subjects they chose; at 3 p.m. he had us all in for half an hour to tell us what was happening at the deep end and to check on what we'd been up to that morning: and at 4 p.m. precisely the stately figure of *The Times* diplomatic correspondent hove into view for a private talk. In those days nearly 50 years ago *The Times*'s foreign policy was thought by all foreign embassies as well as by the Great and the Good on the home front to reflect accurately the views of the Government of the day. Of course *The Times* had many other sources, some much grander than Rids, but if by some mischance *The Times* 'got it wrong' there was great moaning at the bar and Rids had a bad day.

Like all newcomers to the News Department I was completely useless for at least a couple of months. I helped with the business of cutting up the morning newspapers and picking out likely candidates for the daily 'topics' list, sat in with some of the small groups of correspondents at their private briefings and was introduced to more individual customers day after day – I despaired of ever sorting them all out. Peter took me under his wing when he had the time and I made myself useful by reading things to him and learned quite a lot in the process. One of his main interests was the Balkans – in particular the Greek civil war – and he told me to bone up on that. My other new colleagues were also as helpful as they had time to be and I picked up nuggets of wisdom from nearly all of them.

Everyone told me to learn the difference between Ferdy Kuhn, the highly respected, anglophile London correspondent of the *New York Times,* and Freddy Kuh of the *Chicago Tribune,* who was held to be an anglophobe maverick and had new boys like me for breakfast. I was also warned about the dangers of making jokes to customers I didn't know well. The classic example was a long, unfriendly piece by Freddy Kuh which began:

'A Foreign Office spokesman gazed dreamily out of the window across the Horse Guards' Parade and murmured, "Of course one of the troubles with America is that it has no government . . ."'

This naturally caused a first-class rumpus and its onlie begetter, Guy Burgess, who had been in the department for a spell just after the war, was delighted to receive an official raspberry from on high, adding new lustre to his reputation as *enfant terrible*. Guy took both pride and pleasure in annoying establishments of all kinds and 'being in trouble' was a matter for glee rather than anxiety. Rids was greatly relieved when shortly afterwards Guy was removed from the News Department and made an additional Private Secretary to Hector McNeil, the Minister of State. Hector was alleged to have guaranteed Guy's future good conduct. From time to time he would hop off his exalted new perch to visit his old stamping ground, standing at the back of the room at the Twelve Thirty among his former acquaintances and customers, hoping perhaps to be a witness to a stunning new rumpus. Sometimes he would poke his head round our door to see if anyone felt like a gin and peppermint in the Messengers' Bar, a gloomy cavern in the bowels of the building.

Slowly I got the hang of things and eventually I was allowed to take my share of night and weekend duty. News traffic was generally light at these times and there was only one of us on duty. To begin with I sat on the edge of my chair waiting for the worst, but I grew to like the weekend stint, which meant that I got Monday and Tuesday off. As the job wasn't popular with my married colleagues it often came my way. Mostly it was dead quiet but if there was a crisis requiring some reaction from the Foreign Office it was hellish, with all the telephones going at once while one tried to find the right person to authorise some sort of statement. It was as well to keep a close eye on the Reuters tape for early warning of impending trouble, but even so one could still get caught out.

One Sunday evening Reuters carried a piece from Cairo reporting the shooting down of two RAF fighters by Egyptian anti-aircraft guns. The pilots had baled out and were OK. They were giving cover to the last of the British troops leaving Palestine at the end of the Mandate and I was authorised to say that this was an extremely regrettable incident. 'Can't go stronger than that' said the Under-Secretary. 'But we can always beef it up tomorrow when we know how it happened.' Fine. I did everything according to Cocker: rang the Press Association and gave them the statement and did the same for Reuters. The PA piece would be in every British newspaper office within minutes and Reuters would cover the rest of the world. I checked the statement as it came through on Reuters' tape, repeated it to the long waiting queue of callers, shut up shop and went home.

But somehow the PA had managed to mangle my innocuous little statement so that with a few (for me) life-saving exceptions, including *The Times*, all the morning papers quoted a Foreign Office spokesman as saying, 'We very much regret this incident', thus implying an apology for having our fighters shot down. Not quite the same thing and there were inevitably howls of rage, threats of parliamentary questions and it had the makings of a high-class rumpus. The fact that *The Times* 'had it right' as well as Reuters' and a few others to whom I'd spoken myself was good enough for Rids to get the heat turned off and I sat in his office nervous but enthralled as he went to work on it. When he'd done his stuff I thanked him and said I was sorry he'd been troubled. 'For God's sake don't you start apologising. *The Times* had it right, it's your day off – what more could anyone ask?' He added more kindly that if something like this happened again when I was on my own I should ring up him or Norman and share the load.

Sunday afternoon had a particular built-in hazard in the shape of occasional lunatics and, much worse, practical jokers, sober or otherwise, who rounded off their long Sunday lunches by ringing up to try out their impersonations, complete with 'funny voices', of irate Cabinet ministers, silky aides at Buckingham Palace, incomprehensible Far Eastern free-lances and the jokers' favourite – Mr Bevin, the Foreign Secretary himself.

It was a matter of pride not to be taken in by the hoaxers and when, one Sunday afternoon, a caller said, 'Bevin 'ere.' I wasn't too impressed and simply said, 'Oh yes?' The voice explained, plausibly enough, that in the absence of the Minister of Labour abroad he was 'taking an interest' in the settlement of the current dock strike. He'd just heard from Arthur Deakin, the Secretary General of the TUC, that the dockers had at last voted by a show of hands to go back to work the next day. He wanted to be sure that the BBC reported this decision accurately and clearly in their six o'clock bulletin. I was to find out and let him know as soon as possible.

By this time I was sure that this wasn't a hoax and also beginning to wish it was. The duty editor in the BBC news room was a Mr Breathing who fairly politely told me to mind my own business. Warming to his theme he said that the BBC was independent and not a tool of the Government, and in any case the dock strike had nothing to do with the Foreign Office. The fact was that the BBC reporter on the spot said that the show of hands was inconclusive and that was what the six o'clock news would say. I repeated that Mr Bevin's information was that there had been a clear decision to go back to work. Perhaps Mr Breathing would like to speak to Mr Bevin himself? No, he wouldn't, and the BBC couldn't fudge the news to please Mr Bevin or anyone else. He rang off.

It was getting on for five o'clock when I gave Mr Bevin the ill tidings and was told to get a car and get over to Carlton House Terrace quick. On arrival I let the car go and went upstairs to find Mr Bevin in his shirt-sleeves talking to Arthur Deakin on the telephone. He waved me to a chair: 'Now, look 'ere Arthur, my boy Maclean says that won't wash with the BBC. Their man says it wasn't a clear vote to go back and that's what they're going to say on the six o'clock. We've got half an hour to change their minds and you're going to have to make a statement double quick.' Mr Bevin was clearly enjoying himself and I sat transfixed as he marshalled his forces. He got through to the Director General of the BBC and told him that he'd got a national crisis on his hands whether he knew it or not. If the BBC 'got it wrong' it would be solely responsible for prolonging the strike. His head would be on the block. He hunted down the Permanent Under-Secretary at the Ministry of Labour and told him to get over to the BBC, picking up Arthur Deakin on the way. If he hadn't got a car handy he'd send me in the FO car. My heart sank and I had to interrupt to tell him that I'd sent the car back to Downing Street. 'I wish you'd use your 'ead, boy', so 'Cancel that, find your own way.' He had the whole thing buttoned up in a quarter of an hour and he told me to get back to the Office and check that the results of his intervention had filtered through to the BBC news room. I could run if I liked. I scuttled off and rang Mr Breathing again – just to warn him, I said, that Arthur Deakin would be making a statement in time for the six o'clock news. 'I know, I know,' he said and I thought I could detect a faint sigh. I turned on the wireless at six o'clock in time to hear the BBC 'get it right'.

About a week later I happened to be passing the Foreign Secretary's private entrance at the side of the building as Mr Bevin emerged to get into his car. He paused when he saw me and said with a grin, 'We did all right the other day, didn't we?'

When I'd been in the department for eighteen months or so we had a visitation from the Inspectors whose job it was to assess the efficiency, security and costs of every department in London and of every mission abroad.

Rids had been trying for some time to get my salary raised from the

£326 per annum which I'd been offered and accepted when I started in the German Political Department. All my Irregular colleagues were paid a minimum of £600 and he thought I should be paid the same. The Personnel Department had unbent to the tune of another £16 pa, but it seemed that the problem of my age (24) was insoluble. Rids thought that the Inspectors might be persuaded to recommend a change and he told me that when my turn came for an interview I should make it plain that I'd have to look for another job if they didn't put me in for a hefty raise. Privately I had doubts that this would cut any ice and, sure as eggs, when I said my piece the Inspector replied quite kindly that his job was to try to save money, not dish it out to the deserving poor. So it looked as though the end of my brilliantly enjoyable career in 'the Diplomatic' was in sight.

I needed to earn quite a bit more so that I could move out of my mother's comfortably rambling flat in Kensington. Andy and I had been living there, more on than off, for over two years and although she quite liked having us on the premises she couldn't afford to subsidise us for ever and she really wanted to let off our rooms, which would dramatically improve her cash flow. Andy was pining to get back to New Zealand and was temporarily baffling the customers in the ticket office at Wood Green underground station but at least he was paid more than I was. 'Serves you right for being such a baby,' was his view.

Rids called me in to his office soon after our joint failure to impress the Inspectors. Vernon Bartlett, who at that time combined the jobs of Foreign Editor and Diplomatic Correspondent of the *News Chronicle* as well as being an independent MP, was there and he told me that he needed an assistant. Would I be interested? Of course I would. I went to see the Editor of the *News Chronicle,* who said that as far as he was concerned the job was mine but that I would have to get the blessing of the proprietor, Lord Layton. He was a newly created Liberal peer and a former parliamentary colleague of my father's. It all sounded too good to be true and it was.

I still don't know what went wrong at the interview except that I can't remember anything that went right. My arrival in his office was followed by a long silence. He just looked at me for what felt like minutes and then gave a sort of groan. He transferred, his gaze to the large window to one side of his desk and looked out of that. He never looked at me again, so

I suppose enough was enough. He managed to ask me what I'd been doing during the war and thereafter, but my nerve had gone and all I could produce was a brief tentative summary which understandably failed to ignite his interest, so silence descended once more. Eventually he said, 'Thank you for coming to see me' and I slunk away. I saw Vernon a few days later and said I was sorry I'd mucked it up although I didn't know where I'd gone so disastrously wrong. 'I'm sorry too,' he said, 'but it probably wasn't your fault. He's like that sometimes.'

Quite soon I could begin to see the funny side of my failure, much to the relief of my colleagues who'd been holding back on the jokes to spare my wounded feelings. The next day's 'topics' was headed by 'New Job for Alan'.

Guy, who was always on the look-out for News Department gossip, got to hear of this. Had I considered the possibility that Lord Layton had been struck dumb by God, who perhaps wanted me for a Friend? (MI6 were known as The Friends at that time.) He had a friend who was a retired Friend and could easily arrange for me to test my vocation.

I wasn't exactly thrilled by the prospect but I thought I might as well as dip a toe into those murky waters and see what happened. I duly had a drink with Guy's friend and shortly afterwards had a telephone message inviting me to meet a Colonel Scotland at an address in South Kensington. Colonel Scotland looked like a Colonel although I doubt if his name was Scotland. He looked even more like one of Richard Usborne's *Clubland Heroes.* He was in mufti, a light tweed suit, a well-cut collar to his clean white shirt and a regimental tie which I couldn't identify. He was relaxed, friendly and offered me a cigarette from a silver case. So far a great improvement on Lord Layton. He seemed to know quite a lot about me so I didn't have to mumble through my short curriculum vitae.

We chatted amiably for a bit and he then said that he could well understand why I wanted to leave the News Department, a very public sort of job which he gathered I was good at. But he wondered why I thought I should be good in his service, which was very private? For instance I would never be able to tell anyone outside the service what my job was. Would that worry me? I said that it might, but his service was so private that I didn't know what it did nor, of course, how it did it. Could he enlighten me? No, sorry, he couldn't at this stage. Espionage was, like the City of God, both broad and far but the likeness rather stopped there.

Perhaps if I had specific questions he might be able to help. I said that it was difficult to know what to ask but that he would know from my regiment that I wasn't a terrific thruster. If, for instance, the job involved mostly desk work I might be OK at that. But if there were a lot of dashing things to be done then I might not.

'Well,' he said, 'it does rather depend on what you mean by "dashing". What sort of thing did you have in mind?'

I said that if I had, say, to recover the stolen plans and this meant hanging upside down by my toes from a drainpipe then I'd be fairly certain to be a bit of a disappointment to all concerned – except of course the other side.

I wasn't, in fact, joking but the colonel looked as though he thought I might be. 'Perhaps,' he said, 'you'd better think about all this. Why not sleep on it and let me know tomorrow if you'd like to take it further? If so we could get a bit more serious with each other. It's not something about which you can ask advice from family or friends. It's a lonely sort of decision. Some find it a lonely sort of life too. Anyway, here's a telephone number you can ring tomorrow. Just give your name and say yes or no. If it's yes then we'll get in touch with you and you and I can meet again. If it's no then we can both forget all about it.'

That evening I'd arranged to meet James Farmer, now scratching a living by selling an occasional painting, in Soho. Old friends have their uses and it occurred to me that this could be a conclusive test of my ability to keep a secret. James thought that working for the Foreign Office was a very good joke in very bad taste and I knew that he would find the idea of my becoming a secret agent even more hilarious; I wasn't too sure that I wanted to give him that satisfaction. It very nearly worked because he was preoccupied with his own problems. The nice girl he lived with was seriously fed up with him and, unforgivably, seriously critical of his painting.

It wasn't until we'd left the restaurant that James cheered up enough to ask me if I'd found another job and I replied, fatally, 'Not exactly.' I'd given him a blow-by-blow account of my afternoon with Colonel Scotland before we'd reached the bus stop and he'd clearly enjoyed it. I was both relieved and annoyed with myself. 'What happens next?' he asked. 'Nothing,' I said crossly. 'Nothing at all. By telling you I've lost my chance of a great career in the Great Game.'

I didn't tell anyone else about Colonel Scotland but I think that Rids may have known. When he told me that the Personnel Department wanted to second me to Western Organisations Department for a few weeks he said slyly that I'd be glad to know that I wouldn't need to be interviewed for the job. 'Not your strongest suit, I'd say'. I was to work for Evelyn Shuckburgh at the forthcoming meetings with the Americans and the French to get NATO off the ground. Evelyn was to be the Secretary General and he needed two dogsbodies, of which I was one. I was looking rather sulky and when Rids said sharply that it would be valuable experience I said, 'What for?' 'Why, for whatever crops up next, my dear,' was all he cared to say.

This unexpected bout of forced labour turned out to be highly enjoyable and Evelyn was good to work for. He gave me and my fellow conscript each a copy of Eliot's *The Waste Land* and inscribed it 'with affection and admiration' so it seemed that, like Jeeves, we had given satisfaction. At any rate when I got back to the News Department Rids seemed unaccountably pleased with himself and with me and I began to hope that a pay rise was approaching, bringing with it the key to my own bed-sit and a boost to my mother's bank balance.

I didn't have long to wait for good news from the Personnel Department who offered me the choice of two jobs. The first was on the Secretariat of the newly formed Council of Europe, the predecessor of the European Parliament, in Strasbourg. The work didn't sound a laugh-a-minute and I'd have to brush up on my French. But the pay and allowances were at European rates and worked out at nearly six times my present pay with a three-year contract. I said as fast as I could get the words out that I'd accept it but they said, 'Hang on because we've got another job which you ought to think about.' This was to go to New York as Private Secretary to Sir Gladwyn Jebb, who was about to become the UK Permanent Representative at the Security Council and Head of the UK Delegation to the United Nations. I would have the temporary rank and pay of a Second Secretary. Much more interesting, he said, but not so well paid and I'd still be on the same three months' notice on either side. They would probably want to replace me with a Regular after a year but the Press Attaché was due to move on at about that time and I'd be a candidate for that job. No promises, of course. Would I let them have my decision by the end of the week?

I said truthfully that I was amazed. If they wanted to keep me all they had to do was to shell out another couple of hundred pounds a year. Of course I would accept one of these glamorous jobs but I was very happy where I was in the News Department. So why the coals of fire? They said that there were often ways of getting round a brick wall instead of bashing one's head against it. They were simply offering me the choice of two of them.

I hustled back to Rids who said I'd be mad not to go with Gladwyn. 'Not the most popular boy in the school, I know, but he's much easier to work for than with. Ask around.' I did so and received the same piece of advice from everyone. I'd be perfectly all right as long as I never let him think that I was frightened of him. 'Should I be?' I asked. 'Not at all,' they said, 'just remember that he's not devious and that his brusqueness is simply natural bad manners and you'll be fine.'

I found the prospect of New York irresistible but I had to see Gladwyn before either of us was committed. Whatever the outcome my News Department days were over.

As a leaving present Peter asked me if I'd like to take the Twelve Thirty one day during my last week as a Foreign Office spokesman. It would have been ungracious to refuse but I was very nervous all the same. Peter explained to the assembled throng that I was leaving and that this was in the nature of a Hail and Farewell appearance. However, no punches need be pulled and business was as usual.

I took the chair and there was dead silence. No questions. Eventually some kindly soul said, 'Hail' and I said, 'Farewell' and that was that.

Peter said, 'Congratulations. I knew you'd get it right first time!'

'Aw shucks,' I said modestly.

'Oh, I don't know,' he said. 'Think how many brilliant careers are based solely on never getting it wrong. I think you're off to a great start.'

7. Glad About Gladwyn

The prospect of having another go at being a private secretary set off alarm bells in my head. It was three years since my bewildering weeks in Frank Pakenham's private office but this time it would be for real, tied to the tail of a tiger reputed to be a clever, arrogant, ambitious bully. He certainly looked the part – tall, imperious, handsome, a disdainful curve to his mouth – and I could imagine sobbing secretaries and whey-faced subordinates cringing in the presence. It was all very well to be told that I'd be all right if I never let him think that I was frightened of him. He'd see through that soon enough and it seemed to me that my only hope was that, face to face, I actually would feel no fear. I decided that I'd just take things as they came at the interview and if at the end of it I felt either dread or rising panic or both I'd opt for Strasbourg.

The interview was a welcome anti-climax in that Gladwyn clearly regarded the matter as already settled and said that the private secretary job would only be for about a year and would give me time to play myself in for the press attaché job which was really what he wanted me for. We talked about the News Department and he seemed amiable and relaxed. He'd been Private Secretary himself to two Permanent Under-Secretaries, one of whom was Sir Alexander Cadogan whose successor at the UN he was about to be. 'Other people,' he said slyly, 'always think a private secretary has a great deal more influence than he could possibly have. So if you've a fancy for playing the *éminence grise* for the benefit of the credulous you could amuse yourself with that. As long as you don't actually believe it yourself I shan't mind. The important thing is that you'll be my first line of defence against the world and I'm sure you'll quickly learn the best way of keeping the bores at bay.'

No panic, no dread, and it appeared that the decision had already been made without any help from me. So be it, I thought.

Gladwyn's reassuringly casual view of my role in his working life was fine but I thought perhaps the Personnel Department might be more explicit about what the job of a private secretary entailed, so I asked them. Long silence. 'Hard to say really. It's sheepdog stuff.' I asked whether Gladwyn was the shepherd or the sheep. 'Good question. A bit of both you could say. But look in before you go and we'll dredge up a few Dos and Don'ts. It's all common sense and you and Gladwyn will work it out as you go along. But you'll be a working dog, not a domestic pet. That's the main thing.'

I never got my Dos and Don'ts because on Sunday 25 June, a fortnight before we were due to leave on the *Queen Mary*, the North Korean army crossed the 38th Parallel and the Korean War began. The Americans announced that they were sending troops from Japan to support the South Koreans and the Security Council was already in session at Lake Success. Gladwyn's presence was urgently required and we managed to get on to an aeroplane to New York a couple of days later.

In those days transatlantic aeroplanes took their time and we stopped at Dublin, Reykjavik and Gander. We were sustained by what seemed to be an endless succession of breakfast-type snacks. Gladwyn had put his watch back five hours and refused all offers of drinks: 'Too early for me thank you.' We'd been flying for several hours and our third breakfast seemed to be imminent when we were offered quarter bottles of champagne. I thought this was as good a time as any to start on the business of not appearing to be frightened of him and gratefully accepted mine. Gladwyn laughed – an engaging high-pitched sound half-way between a giggle and a titter. 'Do you always drink champagne before breakfast?' I suspected him of having saved this up since Breakfast No. 1 and said, 'Only when it's free.' We settled for that. There was unlimited time for reading, chatting and sleeping and we were in quite good shape when we landed at Idlewild in the early afternoon. We were immediately offered lunch which we politely refused. I added for Gladwyn's benefit, 'Too late for me thank you.'

As soon as we got to the delegation's offices on the 61st floor of the Empire State Building (still at that time the tallest skyscraper in the world), Gladwyn was whisked off into meetings. I was taken on a tour of the premises and introduced to most of my new colleagues, some of whom I already knew. A couple of hours later I was shown Gladwyn's far from palatial office and deposited in my own small nest leading off it.

I have no head for heights and, looking out of the large sash window by my desk, I was horrified to see the tiny L.S. Lowry figures and traffic crawling about below. There was an inward-sloping strip of thick glass about a foot high along the length of the window sill designed, presumably, to prevent papers flying off the desk. It would also have made it a bit more difficult for neurotic inhabitants to take an impulsive leap. Feeling rather faint I backed away wondering how I was going to live with this unexpected hazard. I finally decided to put one leg at a time over the sloping glass obstacle and give it a good shake out in the open air and see if that would do the trick.

I was working on the second leg when I heard the door open behind me and the silky tones of Gladwyn's 'sympathetic' voice: 'Oh dear. So soon?' I gave it a final waggle, shut the window and said 'No, it's just that I don't care for heights and I thought this might help.' 'And does it?' I said that time would tell. 'All right,' he said, 'I've had enough of today so let's go and find a hamburger.'

I left him later at his hotel and walked a few blocks to my less grand establishment. The New York summer air smelled good, the hamburgers had been good and I thought that life with Gladwyn might just be good too.

I got to the office early the next morning anxious to see if my home-made cure for vertigo had worked. I walked over to the window, opened it and looked out and down. Nothing, not a twinge. I was still standing by the window with a fatuous smile on my face when Gladwyn came in. 'Well?' 'It works,' I said proudly. Gladwyn wasn't impressed. 'Don't get too cocky. Remember the old Hays Office ruling about Hollywood bedroom scenes? Keep one foot on the ground at all times.'

After all the fuss of getting to New York on time there wasn't at first a great deal for Gladwyn to do. The crucial resolutions had already been passed by the Security Council before we arrived. North Korea was branded the aggressor and all members of the United Nations were called on to help the South Koreans to repel the invaders. The American decision to send troops, aeroplanes and the Seventh Fleet from Japan was approved and endorsed as the nucleus of the United Nations forces, with General MacArthur named as their Supreme Commander. They were later joined by troops from 16 member nations including Britain, France, Canada, Australia and New Zealand.

None of this decisive action would have been possible if the Russians had not been boycotting the Security Council in protest against the refusal of the West to recognise Mao's Communist China as the rightful occupant of the Chinese seat at the United Nations. They would simply have exercised their right of veto and the usual stalemate preventing any UN action would have ensued. But there we were with a ready-made UN war about to begin and the hapless Soviet delegate, Jakob Malik, sulking in his tent awaiting instructions from Moscow.

Gladwyn spent his time consulting his fellow members of the Security Council, the Commonwealth representatives and the senior members of the Secretariat. This was easy for him because he had been involved in the conception and birth of the UN in 1945 and had been its Acting Secretary-General for a few months in 1946 before the first (and then current) Secretary-General, the many-sided Norwegian Socialist Trygve Lie, was elected. Since then Gladwyn had been the chief Foreign Office adviser on United Nations affairs in London. So he already had many friends (and a few enemies, too) among the delegates and the Secretariat. He slid easily into the swirling waters of the UN pool like some senior sea-lion rejoining the pack after a spell basking on the rocks.

The grand new UN building on the East River in central Manhattan was still in the process of construction and the Security Council meetings were held at the temporary headquarters at the optimistically named Lake Success on Long Island. The journey by car from the Empire State took over an hour on a good day and in the weeks to come when the Security Council was often meeting every day the logistics became inconvenient, complicated and exhausting. Gladwyn's enormous black Cadillac became an extension of our office although car telephones still belonged to the future. He managed to get a lot of reading done and scrawled notes in his flowing illegible handwriting on the various missives which I produced for him. It was all right for him but not so good for me because reading anything in a moving car made me feel sick. He kept a wary eye on my colour and somehow I managed never to get to the dreaded point of throwing up. That would have been high on Personnel Department's list of Don'ts.

Gladwyn's predecessor, Sir Alexander Cadogan, hadn't much cared for New York and regarded the Empire State as a poor substitute for the Foreign Office where he had previously reigned supreme as Permanent Under-Secretary. Accordingly he had rented a large Long Island villa at

Oyster Bay, not far from Lake Success, and worked from there. Gladwyn inherited this sprawling, dank super-bungalow and with it a butler, Gravett, in the great tradition of diplomatic major-domos. This meant that he was intensely loyal to the master (and his family if he approved of them), barely civil to visitors and openly contemptuous of the Office staff no matter what their rank. Gravett reserved a particular loathing for private secretaries, past and present, and lost no time in demonstrating it when Gladwyn and I appeared for the first weekend after our arrival. My predecessor had glibly said that I might find Gravett 'a bit difficult at times', but I was rather taken aback by the depth of his hostility. When he eventually showed me to my bedroom he looked me straight in the eye and said that he had no time for private secretaries and if I thought that I could interfere in his domain I was quite wrong. I asked him why he thought I might want to do that and he simply said, 'You all bloody do' and stumped off.

We were only staying one night and as we were getting ready to drive back to Manhattan on Sunday afternoon Gladwyn told me to make arrangements with Gravett for a dinner party which he wanted to give on the following Saturday. I said I'd do my best but it might be better if he told the old monster himself. He'd warned me off his patch and if it was left to me and Gravett he might end up with a dinner party and no dinner. Gladwyn wanted to know exactly what he'd said and was clearly delighted by Gravett's vituperative gifts. He thought he might mention that he'd been Cadogan's private secretary not so many years ago and that history had a nasty way of repeating itself: Gravett might find himself entrapped as my butler one day. I don't know what passed between them but Gravett and I rubbed along after a fashion until Cynthia, Gladwyn's famously beautiful and strong-minded wife, arrived and took charge. In fact Gravett took to Cynthia and the young Jebbs in a big way and when, after four years in New York, Gladwyn became our Ambassador in Paris he took Gravett with him.

In mid-July Mr Malik, the Soviet delegate, announced that he would return to the Security Council on 1 August for his turn as president. The presidency rotated each month and it would be Gladwyn's turn on 1 September. As president Malik could not rescind or alter the resolutions passed in his absence, but he could set his own agenda, hog the limelight, make lengthy polemical speeches and in propaganda terms try to regain some of the high ground. He had a commanding presence and considerable ability as an orator and debater. The early successes of the North Korean army had been all but conclusive but the rapid build-up of the United Nations forces had prevented a complete rout and it would not be long before MacArthur was driving them back towards the 38th Parallel. Meanwhile Malik would soon be back in place and would use the Soviet veto to prevent any further 'Korean' resolutions by the Security Council. From 1 August fireworks were confidently expected and no one was disappointed.

In 1950 American television technology was still in its infancy although it led the world. It had only recently become possible for the national networks to relay live programmes across the length and breadth of the United States and Canada. The Korean War, the first military action under the banner of the United Nations and led by America, was the prime news topic throughout the country. The networks' decision to relay the proceedings of the Security Council live brought the protagonists into every American home with a television. It was important for the Americans to establish on television that the cause for which their soldiers were already fighting several thousand miles away was just; and to ensure that the forthcoming battle of wits and words at the Security Council was won as well as the real war on the battlefields of Korea.

The snag was that Senator Warren Austin, the American Permanent Representative at the Security Council, was elderly, honest, but with a short fuse to his temper. Malik could and did run rings round him and at times reduced him to near apoplexy of indignation. Neither he nor those who had appointed him the previous year could have foreseen that he would be required to be the leading spokesman for the West in a long-running verbal brawl beneath the television arc lights at Lake Success.

Gladwyn entered the fray like a knight in shining armour and his performance was to match. Short on sound and fury and long on icy clarity and disdain, his speeches and occasional interventions were a class act. His vices as well as his virtues were just what was needed. Arrogance, a caustic wit and a talent for contemptuous demolition of an opponent's argument had made him more enemies than friends among his contemporaries in the past. Now, used against the formidable Malik, they brought him the admiration of millions of American viewers. Within a fortnight he became a modern Mr Valiant-for-Truth, a popular hero second only to Bob Hope in the US television 'personality' ratings. The show was on the road.

Gladwyn was surprised, amused and not too impressed by his sudden fame. Impervious to hostile criticism he was equally unmoved by acclaim and he was neither nervous nor self-conscious about it. He was easily recognised wherever he went and I was relieved to see that when smiling strangers accosted him to shake his hand and pat him on the back he responded politely and cheerfully. I asked him if he was enjoying it. 'Yes,' he said, 'it's a new experience for me, as you may well imagine, and I confess it's rather agreeable. But it won't last forever, so let's hope I don't get a serious taste for it.'

When Malik's month as President was over Gladwyn's love affair with his American fans continued unabated during his own month in the chair. He succeeded in getting the Security Council to invite the South Koreans to attend a Council meeting to give their own account of the North Korean invasion. Naturally Malik objected in forcible terms and tried to claim the right to exercise his veto. But Gladwyn, as president ruled that this was a 'procedural' matter and not therefore subject to veto by any of the five (USA, UK, USSR, France and China) permanent members of the Council. In propaganda terms this was a serious upset for Moscow and Malik, but they were not going to make the mistake of walking out in a huff twice and Malik had to sit and suffer, although not in silence. The South Koreans, waiting in the wings, duly made their appearance and Gladwyn would allow no interruptions. It all made for dramatic television and Gladwyn's presidency ended on a high.

Our tiny office was deluged with fan mail, all of which had to be answered or at least acknowledged. I had been joined by Evelyn James, Gladwyn's PA, and between us we sorted the letters as best we could. We had to use the floor as well as our two desks, leaving a narrow path for Gladwyn and his visitors to get in and out of his office. One hellish morning we were engaged in this unloveable labour when the clasp on Evelyn's necklace broke, scattering pearls in every direction. We were both grovelling on the floor when Gladwyn's door opened and he ushered out the delightful old Indian ambassador, Sir Benegal Rau. As they picked their way through the chaos and escaped into the passage, Sir Benegal asked politely what we were doing. 'I don't know,' said Gladwyn crossly.

'Playing bears, I shouldn't wonder.' I could hear Sir Benegal laughing all the way to the lift.

There were also a great many invitations to speak to institutions and societies, learned and otherwise, and a variety of political bodies. These had to be vetted by the Public Relations pundits of the British Information Services in New York and Washington. He couldn't possibly accept more than a very few at that time and he left it to them to recommend which he should do. The New York expert, Major Bill (later Sir Berkeley) Ormerod, had known Gladwyn and indeed Mr Bevin since 1945 and was rather unkindly referred to by the latter as 'Ormeroids'. Bill lived a life of great social intensity. He 'knew everybody' and 'went everywhere' and had a long-running and successful field-day ensuring that Gladwyn's out-of-town public engagements were 'right'. Gladwyn was genuinely very busy so his speaking engagements had to be fitted in at weekends and this caused unexpected and, I thought, uncalled-for complications with London.

In Britain live television from across the Atlantic was a thing of the future (1962 to be precise) and even ownership of a television set was still a luxury, so Gladwyn's compatriots at home were unable to join in the fun of watching him perform on the box. But his personal success was widely reported and celebrated in the British press and on the BBC. The nation as a whole was pleased but eyebrows were raised in Whitehall. He was doubtless doing a good job – perhaps a spectacularly good job – but was it really 'appropriate' for a civil servant to hit the headlines?

Sir William Strang, the Permanent Under-Secretary at the Foreign Office, clearly regarded Gladwyn's success with deep suspicion and misgiving. In a conversation with Harold Nicolson he said that it was 'bad luck on someone who had done such really serious and important work to become front page news.' Nicolson had of course passed this multilayered remark on to Gladwyn. Having failed to reach Gladwyn on the telephone one weekend Strang sent him a frosty message requesting him to keep London informed of his whereabouts. The rebuke arrived a day or two before Gladwyn was due to go to Philadelphia to speak at a dinner and he was not pleased. 'You'd better ring William up and ask him humbly if I can go.'

I wasn't too fussed by this command because I thought I could get Strang's private secretary to do the actual asking. He could pick a good moment and couch Gladwyn's 'humble' request in suitably non-provocative terms. However, he was too wily to risk getting stuck on our side of the fence and simply said, 'Hang on, I'll ask him.' In the background I could hear Sir William say, 'Put him on the line.' He obviously expected to hear Gladwyn on the other end and was annoyed to find that it was only me. 'Tell Gladwyn that I'm not going to run his life for him and he must judge for himself if this is a good time to be away from his post.' 'Yes, sir.'

I concocted a free translation of this for Gladwyn. Sir William hadn't been too thrilled to have to talk to me but had said that it was entirely up to Gladwyn to go or not to go. So we went and from then on I dutifully sent London a list of Gladwyn's out-of-town speaking engagements with dates and telephone numbers to match.

I don't think Gladwyn ever put a foot wrong in his public performances but this small clash with Strang was the tip of an iceberg of submerged Mandarin disapproval. However, Mr Bevin didn't care whether Gladwyn's success was 'appropriate' or not. He'd always liked, admired and been amused by him and was quoted as saying, 'Say what you like about Gladwyn, but he ain't never dull.' And now he was delighted by the unexpected turn in his career. So Gladwyn's back was covered in Whitehall by the Foreign Secretary himself.

One evening Gladwyn and I had dinner with Mary Barber (later Henderson) who had been the *Time* correspondent in Athens and was now working for them in New York. She said that many of the top editors on *Time* thought that the British Government was dangerously 'soft' on Red China. On the other hand they much admired Gladwyn. Would he come to a working, off-the-record lunch and see if he could clear the air? We'd taken him to a small Greek restaurant and Gladwyn was more interested in trying out his classical Greek on the waiters, who clearly thought he was a lunatic. But it was all very friendly and Gladwyn agreed to face the *Time* firing squad the following week. This proved to be a failure all round and Mary and I composed a few lines of doggerel to mark the occasion:

> We're terribly glad about Gladwyn
> He's had a terrific success
> American house-wives adore him
> And he's had a magnificent Press.

But he's less of a star back in London
Greek waiters consider him mad
And the pundits on *Time* wouldn't spare him a dime
And that's really terribly sad.

As far as I was concerned he wasn't at all hard to work for. He was tolerant of my mistakes, including the time I mixed up the application forms for his driving licence and the car licence for his Cadillac and filled in his colour as 'black with buff upholstery'. The only time I felt hard done by was when he left me in the Empire State waiting for a call from the Secretary-General after a warning was received of an approaching hurricane and he and nearly everyone else went home. 'The boy stood on the burning deck, whence all but he had fled . . .' was how I felt about it. In fact there were three others hanging on for different reasons. The noise of the wind was tremendous but we felt quite safe until some of the plastered ceiling fell down and we opted for a descent. We walked down the emergency stone staircase to the 50th floor where we rashly accepted the offer of a ride in an elevator which was operating at about one tenth of its normal speed. We could hear the side of the car scraping against the steel hawser as it swayed in its shaft and our situation reminded me of those agonising, endless last seconds of a nightmare from which one struggles feebly to awake. To our great credit none of us actually screamed out loud and it felt marvellous to be on the ground.

It's true that Gladwyn didn't like working with subordinates who were afraid of him. I think he found the idea of his own staff being frightened by him both incomprehensible and insulting. There were very few of us who were afflicted in this way but one of the sufferers said that when Gladwyn was near him he felt like a tethered goat and started to bleat. But most of us either knew from past experience or quickly found out that if you stood your ground, were not tempted to show off too much and were not to be bullied into incoherence or frivolity, he was a very good boss.

The annual session of the General Assembly of the United Nations lasted from October 1950 until late January 1951. It was as usual the time when the top political brass of all member nations came to New York to make speeches and the Security Council was no longer the sole arena for verbal battles. In December the forces of Communist China joined the

North Koreans and it soon became clear that the best both sides could hope to achieve was a military stalemate along the 38th Parallel. The danger that the new situation could escalate into a war between the West and Communist China was real enough to bring the Prime Minister (Attlee) to Washington for reassurance that President Truman had no intention of carrying the war beyond the Yalu river into Chinese territory. This was readily forthcoming although the President still had the problem of General MacArthur to solve.

Mr Bevin, already a sick man, was in New York for only a week. He pulled Gladwyn's leg by complaining that his friends assumed that 'he'd only come to bask in Gladwyn's reflected glory'. He died a few months later.

As we moved into the New Year there was still little for the Security Council to do and the international focus was on the Korean battlefield, General MacArthur's Headquarters in Tokyo, the White House in Washington and to a lesser extent Peking, Moscow and London. Gladwyn's heroic role at Lake Success was past history.

The Red China government in Peking had temporarily superseded the Soviet Union as Public Enemy No. 1 in the eyes of the American public and the fact that Britain, along with most of the Commonwealth and France, had recognised Mao's government over a year previously became a sore point. America still recognised Chiang Kai-shek's government holed up in Taiwan and there could be no chance of that changing after Red China's troops had come in on the side of North Korea. The same deadlock applied to the Chinese seat at the United Nations which included a permanent (with right of veto) seat at the Security Council. It was not resolved in favour of Communist China until President Nixon established diplomatic relations with Mao's government in 1972. For now it was enough that the West was united in its aim of containing the war and re-establishing the border between North and South Korea with a 'buffer zone' manned by United Nations troops on either side of it. It took nearly two years to achieve this.

Gladwyn was still much in demand as a speaker but confined himself to trying to get over to his audiences the limitations of what the United Nations could do in the absence of agreement among the Great Powers. It was a down-beat message but he did it well enough.

The Public Relations advisers were beginning to worry about his public image. There was, they said, a widespread feeling that he was extending the rapier wit treatment to friend as well as foe. They couldn't bring themselves to be specific about Gladwyn's lapses from well-mannered grace but, at the small meeting in the Minister's office to which I was invited, they said they thought that someone should 'have a word' with him. Bill Ormerod, who had a large expensive ear to the ground of New York Society, was nodding his head in a maddeningly responsible way and I suddenly realised that they were all looking at me. Bill said that Americans were very sensitive to slights and set a high value on courtesy. I said that I hadn't observed anything approaching rudeness to anyone outside the office and if he were to demand an example I wouldn't be able to give him one. If someone had to raise it with Gladwyn why not Bill? He was the PR expert. No, Bill wouldn't. I appealed to the Minister, who slowly shook his head, grinned and said, 'This is what private secretaries are paid for.' I thought for a bit and then told them that if I were Gladwyn I'd want to know exactly what I was accused of and by whom. I'd try to keep them out of it but my heart wouldn't be in it and I couldn't make any promises. I hoped that would at least make Bill sweat a bit.

I thought it was best to do it quickly and went straight into Gladwyn's office where he was in his shirt sleeves reading some telegrams. I said that I had something to say which I thought he wouldn't much like. Could I go ahead and say it? Gladwyn leaned back in his chair. 'Yes, do. I'm all ears.'

I told him that there was a general feeling that he wasn't being nice enough to his UN colleagues, particularly the Americans, and there was a danger of hurt feelings turning into resentment. Could he go a bit easy on them?

'Really?' he said 'You amaze me. But thanks for telling me and I'll try to do better.' I felt quite weak with relief and he looked like the cat who'd swallowed the cream.

Not long afterwards he mentioned casually that he had told London that he wanted me to succeed the Press Attaché whose three-year stint would be up in July. The job carried the rank and pay of a First Secretary so for the first time in my life my financial prospects were quite bright. I hadn't realised that I'd been playing for such high stakes. In April 1951 I had the formal letter from the Personnel Department offering me the job, which I accepted.

*

Frank Tuohy, whose books I was to publish at Macmillan a few years later, had been appointed Professor of English Literature at São Paulo University at the end of 1949. He had rather rashly said in a letter to James Farmer that he was enjoying the job and that it was an extremely agreeable place in which to be. James, broke and fed up with carting his pictures round the London galleries to no avail, decided that he would like to go and stay with Frank for a month or two and try his luck in Brazil. James persuaded his father to stand him the price of a (one-way) ticket on a small ship and set forth in the spring of 1950. He cunningly omitted to tell Frank, who had only been there for a few months, of his intentions and it was left to me to send him a cable after the ship had sailed – 'James arrives Santos May 18th. Please meet.'

Frank was understandably annoyed and sent James a cable to the ship: 'Conditions unfavourable. Suggest return immediately,' which made him feel better. But he met the ship and James stayed for nearly a year. In that time he tried his hand at teaching English without too much success but also produced a large number of paintings and drawings.

I shouldn't have been too surprised (but I was) to get a cable from Frank which read, 'Columbus arrives New York Sunday week. Please meet.' I had a faint hope that he might be bringing enough money to support himself for a bit, so I cabled back, 'Columbus welcome. Indians friendly but bring beads.' Frank replied, 'No beads but many pictures.'

I couldn't complain. It was clearly my turn to play host to our old friend and at least Manhattan was blessed with many small galleries and an exhibition might be on the cards.

When two other well-wishers and I had seen James off at Southampton he had an enormous brown beard and very little hair on his head. His passport photograph looked decidedly sinister and his clothes had seen better days. I nearly missed him as he came down the gangplank at the New York docks, failing at first sight to recognise the clean-shaven, smartly dressed figure waving a tentative greeting. 'Spruce' was the word which came to mind. He had little baggage except for two large crates of canvases and portfolios of drawings. I had a spare room in my flat so he was at least guaranteed a roof over his head and he had a few acquaintances of his own in Manhattan. Luckily some of my friends who liked him and admired his pictures set about finding a gallery which might make him solvent, if not famous. Remembering James's problems with London galleries ('greedy, ignorant bastards', etc), I wasn't over-confident. But the Brazilian pictures were good and some of the drawings were stunning. Within a few weeks he had the offer of an exhibition at a small gallery in mid-town Manhattan to open in June. Meantime I used to leave him a dollar for lunch when I departed for work in the morning. Lack of cash was a state to which he was accustomed. There was a lot of work for him to do at and for the gallery with the exhibition only six weeks away; he sold a picture in advance which cheered him up and me too.

The fighting in Korea during February and March was bitter but indecisive and MacArthur was engaged in an equally bitter battle with his own Commander-in-Chief, President Truman. The General believed passionately in 'total victory' and that could mean, among other things, massive bombing of the Red Chinese beyond the Yalu river, a naval blockade of China itself and the dropping of radioactive waste material across the enemy's supply lines. His plans were wild and on 11 April President Truman sacked him. Up to the 38th Parallel he had been a brave and brilliant military commander, beyond it he had become a dangerous political lunatic. He had a vast personal following across the country and he returned home to make a triumphant Progress from the West Coast to the East ending up with a personal hearing by Congress in Washington and a ticker-tape parade covering 19 miles through the streets of Manhattan. The procession passed by the Empire State Building and it was an amazing sight from our lofty windows. It was estimated by the Police Department that 7½ million New Yorkers (compared with four million for Eisenhower in 1945) were on the streets to greet him. The Department of Sanitation's statistics were even more precise, reporting the amount of paper collected from the streets on the route of the motorcade as 3249 tons. This nearly doubled the previous record set by the triumph awarded to Charles Lindberg in 1927.

The sacking of MacArthur did nothing to allay American fears that the British Government was fundamentally unsound on the question of Communist China and for some time an English accent became something to slur in public places.

Gladwyn was going away for a holiday in May and suggested that I might like to take a couple of weeks off at about the same time. My successor would be arriving in June and I would be taking over as Press Attaché in July.

I celebrated my first holiday morning by having my hair cut. The barber was out of sorts and I detected a streak of venom in his scissor-work. It didn't, however, interrupt the flow of his monologue on the evils of those 'Commie bastards in Peking'. From time to time I grunted my agreement in what I hoped was an All-American accent. But he'd already rumbled my origins.

'You're English, huh?'

'Yes.'

'What you doing here?'

I didn't feel like telling him that I was working for the British Delegation to the United Nations. I thought I might lose an earlobe. So I said I was a publisher and six months later I was.

8. *Dear Old Jim*

James and I were staying with friends on the New Jersey coast for the first week of my holiday when the Minister rang up from the office. I was to come back at once. 'Why?' 'Can't tell you on the telephone. Just come.' I asked if this was the end of my holiday and he said he was afraid it was. So I gave James a cheque for $50 to keep him afloat, packed my bag and went.

The telegram to New York, decoded by the Minister in Gladwyn's absence, had only said, 'Donald Maclean disappeared. Fear another breakdown. Send Alan back immediately.' We agreed, the Minister and I, that whatever it was it didn't look too good. I managed to catch the next plane and eight or nine hours later we landed at Prestwick in Scotland to clear Customs and Immigration. The sight of my passport sent the officials into an excited huddle and I watched their important, responsible expressions as they conferred. They hived me off into a small room.

'Are you Mr Alan Duart Maclean?'

'Yes, I am.'

'Do you know a Mr *Donald* Duart Maclean?'

'Yes, of course I do. He's my brother. That's why I'm here. I think.'

They left me and I could hear a drone of discussion, but none of the words, through the partition wall. Quite soon they thanked me, called me 'Sir' in fairly heavily inverted commas and we continued our journey on the last short leg to London.

As I emerged from the plane door on to the steps and into the sunlight I thought of rabbits ferreted out of their burrows into first the blinding light and then the waiting nets and looked round anxiously for a familiar face. Sure enough there was Henry Davidson, the assistant in the Personnel Department, at the bottom of the steps. He didn't smile when he saw me but at least he waved. And then the blandest of greetings. Good flight? Had summer come to New York? Gladwyn going strong?

Yes, yes and yes. We got into the enormous black Daimler waiting for us nearby and purred off, sitting silently side by side, looking out of our opposite windows. As we joined the stream of London-bound traffic, I said diffidently, 'I don't want to be nosey, but what am I doing here? The Immigration people at Prestwick didn't actually put me in a strait-jacket but they looked as though they thought I was a danger to mankind.'

'Oh. Heavens. Well. Yes. Sorry. The thing is that Donald seems to have wandered off God knows where and we haven't a clue where he is. Very worrying for your mother and we thought it would be nice for her to have you with her . . .' I looked at Henry's gentle face and thought, 'They're not arresting me, they're just going to kill me.'

'And what now, Henry?'

'Ah. Yes. Well. Perhaps if you could spare half an hour, you would have a word with one of our chaps in the office before going home?'

'Of course.'

Henry left me on a leather sofa in the first floor corridor of the house in Carlton House Terrace in which the Personnel and Administrative Departments of the FO had their nests. A lovely staircase and a lot of stone and marble. I had sat there a year before when they'd decided to send me to New York. Henry reappeared and ushered me into the presence of a small, furry, pipe-smoking, black-moustached man who shook me warmly by the hand. Henry vanished. This was it. Man to man, cat to mouse, stoat to rabbit.

'Seddon's my name. Jim Seddon.' He sounded rather tentative as if he didn't really think there was much chance that I'd be taken in by such an obvious fib. It sounded all right to me.

Affability was all and I relaxed as we smoked and chatted a bit about the perils and delights of New York, the UN, my job as Press Attaché, and then ranging further back in my short career – to the war, Berlin and the News Department. Had I been in the News Department with Guy Burgess? No. I knew him of course. Who didn't?

Perhaps Mr Seddon was never going to get round to Donald and I began to wonder too if Guy was in one of his well-known 'scrapes'. It'll be my mother and her 'worryings' next, I thought. Sure enough Mr Seddon, as if in tune with the pattern of our emerging relationship, said almost at once that my mother was a wonderfully courageous lady of great charm and possessed of the twin gifts of perceptiveness and intuition. She must also have been a great beauty and indeed retained that beauty in old age. I wondered what on earth my old mother had been up to, almost as much as I wondered what had happened to Donald. I hadn't seen either of them for a year but it sounded as if she wasn't in exactly a state of collapse. Nor would I have expected her to be. She had a will and nerves of iron and steel and was by no means averse to a bit of high drama.

My mother thus established as the great White Queen round which we could lay the worrying pieces of the puzzle of the disappearance of her errant, but not for certain erring son, Mr Seddon told me the events of the previous weekend, as they'd been reported by Donald's wife, Melinda. Briefly, Donald had brought a friend (whom Melinda had not met before) home to supper on Friday evening. He said that they had to go and see another friend or colleague and might well stay the night. He therefore took an overnight bag with him and was seen no more. When he failed to return or telephone on Saturday or Sunday she was worried, but thought glumly that he'd gone out on a bat. She rang the Foreign Office on Monday morning to see if he'd turned up for work and the alarm bells had been ringing ever since.

Mr Seddon confided that all ports and airports were on the look-out for him and that he'd heard within the last few hours that he'd probably taken the night ferry to France from Southampton on Friday. If so, there might possibly be a simple and unworrying explanation for the journey. Or he might be in the throes of another nervous breakdown. But of course there was the mystery of the strange friend with whom he'd departed and who might still be with him, wherever that might be.

'Do you know a man called Roger Styles? Or is the name familiar in any way?'

'No. No.'

A long pause. It was rather like Thurber's court-room cartoon of the DA holding up a small kangaroo by its ears and saying to the cowering witness, 'Perhaps this will refresh your memory!' Jim scuffled through some papers on the desk and produced a photograph which he held at arm's length almost under my nose.

'Recognise him now?' he said quietly.

'Why that's Guy Burgess!' I exclaimed right on cue. 'The mysterious stranger?'

Jim nodded. 'The very same. Now why would he have called himself that, do you think?'

'No idea.'

The ensuing silence in the tobacco haze was somehow triumphant. We had both performed well. After that we gossiped about Guy and the oddness of him and Donald going anywhere together. They hadn't as far as I knew been particularly friendly since their Cambridge days when their zeal for the Party had led them to try to bring a lot of scandalised Trinity Hall College servants out on strike. I remembered Guy telling the story in a pub and saying rather maliciously, I thought at the time, that no doubt Donald would prefer to forget things like that now that he was so strenuously working for his Knighthood.

Our amateur dramatics over for the moment at any rate, Jim promised to keep in close touch and sent his regards to my mother.

'Better not tell anyone you're here,' said Henry, who had shimmered in as I was leaving. I said that I had no English money. Would it be all right if I walked across to the Travellers to cash a cheque? It was lunch time and likely to be full of Foreign Office persons.

'Oh. Yes. Well. That would be all right. But try not to speak to anyone. We don't want the Press in on this.'

Two days later the Case of The Missing Diplomats was premiered in the columns of the *Daily Express* and played to packed houses everywhere for many years.

The Missing Diplomats, M & B, B & M, The Great Spy Scandal, The Cambridge Spies – Treachery, Drunken Debauchery, Homosexuality, The Establishment riddled with traitors to the country and to itself, the Foreign Office bosom crawling with nursed vipers. What a mix, what a story and what a gift to the Press! The great strength of the story was that there were very few hard facts to fetter the ideas and fantasies of journalists who were under considerable pressure to produce new angles and new theories every day. Neither the Government nor the Foreign Office had anything to say one way or the other and their placid denials that they had any idea where their chicks had strayed to added fuel to the fire of speculation. The telegrams from Guy to his mother and from Donald to his wife and to his mother, and the fact that they had been handed in at a Paris post office, were common knowledge. It was also confirmed that they had indeed caught the Cross-Channel ferry on that Friday night. But those facts apart it was a free-for-all with only one common and uncontested basis – that they had defected or were en route to defecting to the

Soviet Union. There were sightings all over Europe and the game of Hunt the Diplomats gave daily pleasure to millions of innocent people.

Naturally it didn't give us, the families and close friends of M & B, anything like the same pleasure and Melinda's life was further complicated by the approaching birth of her third child. Most reporters working on the London end of the story telephoned to all of us once or twice every day and for some weeks we were at times besieged. It was a bewildering time, particularly for Donald and Melinda's small sons.

But there was only limited mileage in getting the same sort of negative responses from the immediate families, and, quite soon, friends, acquaintances, fortune-tellers, those experts who can diagnose character from handwriting and a host of new experts on the psychology of treachery were regularly in print, building up composite and ever-enlarging portraits of the missing persons. And pretty horrific they were. Of the two, Guy's developing profile was much the more rewarding, partly because he had for years taken a mischief-loaded pleasure in recounting his own sexual and political indiscretions in lurid terms to anyone who cared to listen and his conversation, whether of a confessional nature or not, was studded with names dropped and often scattered. The crashing fall from grace of Donald, the blue-eyed boy of the FO, son of a dead and much-respected Liberal Cabinet Minister and all that, was good copy in its own right, but it was the link, now forged for ever, with Guy's own projection of himself as the brilliant but wicked, filthy but fascinating, witty but dangerous man of affairs, that made them such a splendidly evil partnership. As Guy said many years later to Coral Browne in Moscow, 'So awful and boring being chained to poor Donald like Marshall to Snelgrove.'

The Great Flit was the beginning of a savage rent in the fabric of Mandarin society. Overnight, the unthinkable became intoxicatingly thinkable. Civil Servants and particularly Foreign Servants had been allowed and even encouraged to be eccentric in manners, tastes and habits. But this latitude was because they were known to be clever, efficient, highly professional, unconnected in any dangerous way to any of the political parties, and completely loyal to the Crown and to the policies of the Government of the day. All those comfortable assumptions went out of the window and 'mole-spotting' was still a popular sport in the 1980s. It was of course given a terrific boost by the exposure of the deal made by MI5 with Anthony Blunt and various other minor Civil Service characters. The late Sir Roger Hollis was still being pursued until recently by some who, like old-fashioned, over-excited children, clamour for one more game before bed-time. Our current nannies don't seem inclined to be too indulgent on this point.

But in 1951 it was all new and thrilling. I thought at the time, and looking back, still think, that Donald's friends treated him much better than Guy's. Perhaps neither of them deserved much loyalty from the friends they had deceived for so long, but it was sad and unedifying to see someone of the literary, political and social clout of Harold Nicolson impelled to leap on to the band-wagon of the hour to disown publicly his long friendship with Guy. A great many people must have been quite frightened, not because they had been involved in espionage or political indiscretion with or for the Russians in any way at all, but simply because they feared that their friendship with either or both of the two would make them liable to guilt by association. But they were wrong and there wasn't a witch-hunt or anything like one. When you think that at this same time McCarthyism was sweeping America in the wake of the Alger Hiss trial, we can count ourselves lucky that sufferings of the innocent and the ignorant were both rare and accidental.

My own paranoia was of modest proportions and the cat and mouse games between Jim and myself were in fact largely invented by me even though he, unintentionally I'm sure (I think), contributed to them on one or two occasions. At those times I should have been glad to have had the information – given to me later by a friend from Army days who had been working in MI5 – that although my file was six inches thick it had taken only 36 hours to clear me.

All through that summer Jim 'kept in touch' and we became friends of a working sort. He was a nice, unpretentious and even cosy man who got on famously with my mother. They made each other laugh and he never said a nasty thing about Donald to her – or to me for that matter. He was considerate in many small ways, and made her path through the woods less thorny and less dark. I realised that she had only fully adjusted, to her liking, to her new status as mother of a famous traitor instead of a widow of a distinguished politician when I overheard her some years later say to an acquaintance, 'Ah, yes, that was before my son, Donald, went out to Russia.'

It was, however, only a few weeks after my first meeting with Jim that he rang up to say that it was important for us to meet and would I come to Carlton House Terrace? He had so far kept up the pretence that they might still be found lolling on some Ruritanian beach, but I never thought his heart was in it and I couldn't see the point of his faithful reports of remote sightings. This sounded more like the real stuff and it made me nervous.

Jim was waiting for me on the pavement and asked me if I'd mind getting into the back of his car with him. I minded very much. I'd seen too many movies in which people who were invited to get into the backs of cars with people like Jim ended up in handcuffs or even in the river with cement boots on. Or maybe he'd caught Donald and wanted me to be sitting comfortably in case I felt faint?

There was a bit of throat-clearing and puffing on his pipe and then he said there was something he had to tell me. He'd rather tell me than my mother or Melinda but he hoped that I would, if I thought fit, tell them myself in my own time. He didn't want to deceive us any longer. A very long pause. This was it.

'My name is not Seddon. My name is Skardon.'

To remain silent or, worse, to admit that the name meant absolutely nothing to me would be the dirtiest trick a mouse could play on a cat. I managed to say 'Oh' and a little later 'Gosh.'

'You realise that I was the man who persuaded Klaus Fuchs to confess. A dear man. I knew it couldn't be long before you put two and two together.'

I don't know what prompted Jim's confession but he told me that what prompted 'dear old Klaus' to confess was plain old-fashioned kindness. It occurred to me that perhaps confession was the only graceful way of repaying all the kindness which Jim had so far shown us but he seemed quite content with the thanks which was all I had to offer. I think he genuinely felt uncomfortable at the thought of being unmasked. Possibly he feared my mother might fall out of love with him. But in fact if he'd said that MI5 officers used a different name for each case or even for each day of the week we'd have believed him quite happily.

The following week Jim and I were having a drink in a pub and he'd been telling me more about the rise and fall of 'dear old Klaus'. He then said it was a funny old world. Quite a few people had come forward in the last week or so and told him that they'd made damn fools of themselves by, well, giving information to the Russians when they shouldn't have. If I saw what he meant. I wasn't at all sure that I saw what he meant but I certainly didn't like the look of it. Did he, I asked, mean civil servants? Yes, he did. Some quite senior people who should have known better.

'And what have you done with them?'

'Oh,' said Jim airily waving his pipe, 'some have retired from the Service and some have just been transferred to other Ministries.'

'Is that all? I thought they might be joining dear old Klaus at the mail-bags – all broken down by your relentless kindness.'

'Oh no, nothing like that.' Jim seemed really amused and also a bit flattered. 'I don't think they'll do it again.'

I was amazed, rather frightened and when I'd had time to think about it, insulted too. If you wanted someone to confess to treason surely this sort of patently untrue rigmarole about being transferred to the Min of Ag and Fish with a gentle smiling reproof wouldn't deceive even the most gullible of repentant traitors. I said nothing and we soon chatted about other things and he never referred to it again. But, of course, I did him an injustice. After the great rumpus about Anthony Blunt in 1979 former civil servants popped up all over the place and admitted that they too had given classified information to the Russians at one time or another and had indeed been retired or transferred to other Ministries, just as Jim had told me in the pub.

Because he had become our friend, was our only consistent link with 'the Authorities' and was always available for advice or just a chat, I never really thought of Jim in relation to Guy's mother, brother and friends. He belonged to us. But of course he must have been just as important to them as he was to us. It had never seemed appropriate or sensible to make contact with Guy's family. What on earth could we have found to say to each other? But one morning Jim rang up very jolly, to say that I could now collect Donald's belongings which he had left on the Cross Channel ferry. MI5 no longer needed them. He mentioned, a shade too casually, that as all their belongings were mixed up it would be sensible if Colonel Basset, Guy's step-father, and I went together to Waterloo Station and picked out our respective family treasures. An office car would collect me and pick up the Colonel on the way to the station, where the Station Master would receive us. The stuff was now Lost Property, not Evidence.

My own clothes were still on a slow boat from New York and I only had the one suit I'd arrived in. My mother was adamant that I must look at least clean and presentable to do battle with the official Opposition.

She lent me £15 to buy a new suit from Barkers and I went off smelling of new grey flannel and some old Honey and Flowers Brilliantine which had belonged to my father. He died in 1932 and the lotion looked as if it had been fermenting for the last nineteen years. It didn't smell exactly disgusting but I said, correctly as it turned out, that the Colonel would smell better. But otherwise she was quite right. The Colonel was dressed for war – impeccably pin-striped, complete with bowler and rolled umbrella and just a whiff of expensive aftershave. Jim was in attendance, silent and smiling, and I don't remember a single word he said. He was clearly bent on enjoying the outing and would leave the Colonel and me to provide the entertainment.

We were met by a very grand Station Master who led us upstairs to his vast gloomy office. He seemed both excited and embarrassed.

'If you gentlemen would just like to . . . er . . . select your . . . er . . .' His voice trailed off. The Colonel and I stood facing each other across a large table on which were two canvas bags with leather grips and various piles of sad-looking objects and clothes.

'You go first, Colonel,' I said respectfully.

'No,' he said. 'We'll do it fair. Turn and turn about.'

Speed and decisiveness were the thing and we chose entirely at random without a moment's hesitation when our turns came. We got through in what must have been record time until we were left with only two items, either of which might have got the award for the least desirable object in the room – perhaps in the world. The first was a pair of really dirty, torn black pyjamas and the other a revolting pair of socks which were quite stiff with dried sweat and had holes in heels and toes. I was sure that they were both Guy's and said so. The Colonel was equally sure that they were both 'Your chap's'.

I had my one moment of inspiration.

'Donald never wore pyjamas,' I said. 'A sin against Nature, he once told me.' Worthy of Jeeves, I thought, and unless the Colonel was going to admit to an intimate knowledge of Guy's sleeping habits, he was done for. He paused for a moment closed his eyes, opened them and accepted defeat like the gentleman he was.

'Right,' he said, hooking the pyjamas into his bag with the handle of his umbrella, 'but you're having those bloody socks.'

We said goodbye to the Station Master and followed Jim out to the car. On the way I saw a large wire-meshed receptacle.

'Colonel,' I said, 'look!'

'Good man,' he said and both pyjamas and socks went to their long home.

We dropped the Colonel at his club in St James's Street. As we shook hands he nearly smiled, but thought better of it.

'I hope you've enjoyed your morning, Jim.'

He sighed. 'I've had a *lovely* time.'

There weren't many lovely times that summer. It's surprising how quickly you can adapt from a regular, quite hard-working life in an office job to a state of almost total uncertainty in which there is no point in looking more than a few days ahead at any one time. It's true, too, that the pace is slower the nearer you are to the centre of a merry-go-round. There was nothing we could do to influence the course of events. We were reeds shaken by the wind and between gusts we had, like those mythical children in the good old bad old pre-telly days, to make our own amusements. Some of these were a bit silly.

James was back in England. After I'd left for London he went back to my flat in New York before moving on to lodge with another friend. He had a surprise meeting with Cynthia Jebb who assumed that my flat was empty and had arranged a morning appointment with her dressmaker there (Gladwyn had opted for a large house on the Hudson River and they had no base in the city). James, a late riser, heard voices in the sitting-room and came shambling out of his bedroom to investigate. The dressmaker had a mouthful of pins, Cynthia had few clothes on and James had none at all. He looked like a gorilla and the meeting adjourned itself *sine die*.

The exhibition was quite successful, with good reviews and enough pictures sold to buy another one-way ticket, this time on a slow boat to England. Once aboard James was befriended by a rich and (he claimed) beautiful young widow and he arrived in funds and in love. Sadly neither state lasted for very long. But it was good for my morale to see him again and to take heart from his disinclination to take 'serious' things seriously.

We used to play Shake the Tail in and around Kensington – meeting furtively in pubs, switching folded newspapers, leaping on to passing buses and leaping off again at the traffic lights and scuttling through Barkers Food Department out through Ladies Accessories and thence by different routes to the Roof Garden on the top of Derry and Toms. The

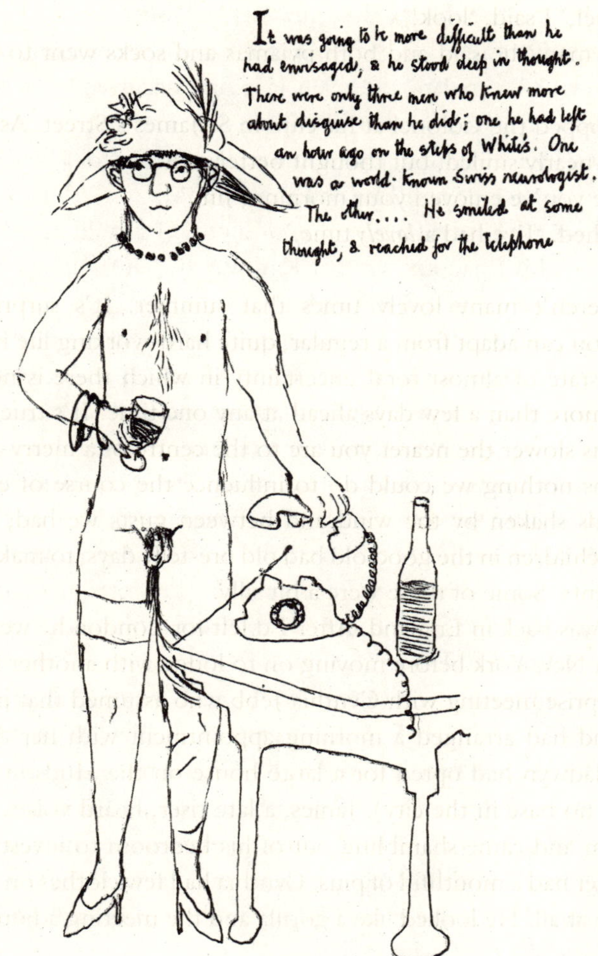

drawing above is taken from a letter he wrote to me at about that time. His handwritten caption reads, 'It was going to be more difficult than he had envisaged, and he stood deep in thought. There were only three men who knew more about disguise than he did; one he had left an hour ago on the steps of White's. One was a world-known Swiss neurologist. The other . . . He smiled at some thought, and reached for the telephone.'

There were already rumblings about a Third Man and this began to make sense of a particularly gnomic instruction which Jim had given me quite early on. 'I must ask you,' he said, tilting his head and puffing on his pipe, 'on no account to try to see Kim Philby. Please don't ask me why.'

'Well, that's no problem. I've only met him once,' I said huffily.

It's always irritating to be told not to do something which you wouldn't have wanted to do, even if it had occurred to you that you could. The implication is that you have only just been prevented from committing mortal sin or at least some reckless act of folly by the wise and timely intervention of an Elder and Better. In this case there is no doubt that Jim's warning me off was meant kindly and I should have been much less ungrateful if I had known that Kim was at that time being grilled in some prosaic dungeon in Whitehall.

Someone, in later life, said to me quite casually, 'It must have been hell at that time, knowing that all your friends thought you were a Communist spy.' I was surprised and rather indignant. It hadn't entered my head that that was what they were thinking. It's true that I once overheard a man in a pub who'd been reading his *Daily Express* say to his companion, 'Of course you can tell that the old mother is in it up to her neck – and that young brother too.' But that seemed rather a joke. It appeared that all my friends both inside and outside the Foreign Office were as friendly and helpful as before, and if they were harbouring these dark suspicions then I'm glad I didn't know.

My relationship with my employers, the Foreign Office, was much more ambiguous. Clearly I couldn't go back to New York. It was quite obvious that Donald had defected to Russia and my presence on the staff of any mission abroad or in any department of the Foreign Office itself could only have been an embarrassment and possibly a dangerous one at that. Supposing They threatened to send me one of Donald's fingernails unless I handed over The Plans. Or any more sophisticated scenario you like. So there was no argument about whether to stay or go. I was going. But as I was only a Temporary Civil Servant on a post-by-post contract, terminable on either side at three months' notice, I could either resign or simply not have my contract renewed. There was a further phrase in it which read '. . . three months' notice or such shorter period as the exigencies of the Public Service may demand.' Well, this was an exigency all right. The only snag was that the FO was still saying both publicly, and privately to me, that they had no idea where Donald was and would draw no conclusions. They urged me to resign, offering a glowing reference and a modest gratuity. Looking back I can't quite see what made me so cross. True it was falling to me to say, at least by implication, that Donald was a defector when they were not prepared to say so themselves. But this was really just sophistry and I knew it. I think it was the expression on the face of the man who was doing the urging (not dear old Henry, I'm glad to say). There looked to be a bad smell under his nose and it was me. Jim was unexpectedly and uncharacteristically militant, egging me on. 'Make them work for their money!' was his advice.

In the end I gave in. My problem came to the notice of Lady Violet Bonham Carter who was a great Liberal friend of my late father and of my mother. She liked a good cause to fight and said she would help me in any way she could. First step would be a Parliamentary Question, ideally to be asked by Churchill, then in Opposition. I knew at once that to become a party political bone of contention would be fatal to my chances of getting another job, and I resigned within the hour.

The reference was indeed glowing and a version of it appeared in *The Times* too. The £350 came in very handy and I thought seriously of giving my mother back the £15 she'd 'lent' me for my Waterloo suit.

My mother had never gambled or backed a horse in her life. But in 1954 she gave me ten shillings with the instruction to put it on a horse called Never Say Die, ridden by an unsmiling 18-year-old Lester Piggott, which was a 14-1 shot for the Derby. It duly won and she accepted her winnings proudly. 'There,' she said. 'What did I tell you?' This was the nearest she ever got to admitting that we had anything more daunting than one of Harold Macmillan's 'little local difficulties' on our hands. Her loyalty to and confidence in her brood were absolute and although she was too old and infirm to make the journey to Moscow when that became possible, she corresponded with Donald regularly up to the time of her death in 1962.

Moscow, 1983

As we, the dozen or so passengers on the British Airways flight, emerged from the plastic tunnel, I could see what looked like a vast maze of long glass corridors. As we trudged through them, we came up a long incline towards a lighted and populated area. Then I saw a shorter corridor forking left and two waiting figures – one tall and stooped and the other short and stout. Both wore fur hats. They gave no sign but I drifted left and almost at once Donald and I were reunited in a bear hug and I was introduced to 'my friend Vassily'. On the aeroplane I'd wondered if I might meet someone like Vassily, in which case I could say, 'Are you my brother's keeper?' but my nerve failed me, the moment passed and another bad joke was stillborn. Vassily led us through a side door. We walked slowly because Donald used a stick. He looked not too bad, a bit grey in the bright airport lights. We held hands rather shyly like children. It was going to be all right.

Donald and I sat in the back of the small black car and I was quite unprepared for the racing start. We swished through the airport approach roads, sending up great waves of icy slush and hurtled through traffic lights, green or red. Donald spoke urgently in Russian to Vassily who turned, smiled and shrugged. Donald said to me, 'They've no right to do this' and for a few awful moments I was paranoid again and back with Henry in the Daimler on the road to London in 1951. In my mind's eye I could see the cold dirty white-tiled passages of the lunatic asylum awaiting us. But he was only protesting at the terrifying arrogance of the young KGB man's driving. 'An ugly symptom,' he said.

He had not long to live and we had three days to catch up. We talked greedily for hours that evening – mostly about our childhoods, separated by 12 years. As we said good night and were slouching off to our lairs I had the feeling that in his head he was still 19, embarking instead of disembarking. 'You're not meant to have grey hair,' he said.

I turned back at the door to my room. He had promised not to tell me anything which Jim and his successors did not already know, and for that I was truly thankful. But I said there was only one thing I'd wanted to know for 32 years and hoped he could see his way . . .

For a moment he looked aghast.

'Why did Guy call himself Roger Styles?'

'Oh, *that*.' He smiled. 'He'd brought a couple of old green Penguins with him. Agatha Christies – *The Mysterious Affair at Styles* and *The Murder of Roger Ackroyd*. Happy?'

'Yes. Very. Thanks.'

Dear old Roger. Dear old Jim.

9. *Billy Collins Isn't It?*

After I'd resigned I was wondering whether I was employable in any way unconnected to the rumpus when a letter arrived from Mark Bonham Carter, Violet's elder son and a friend from childhood. Would I be interested in a job at Collins where he was working as an editor? If so would I come to see Billy Collins, the firm's Chairman? The job would be in Glasgow.

I went to the Collins London office in St James's Place where Billy told me that his brother Ian, the Vice-Chairman who ran the Glasgow end of the business, was looking for an assistant. Ian could see me the day after tomorrow and they'd pay my fare. 'Go up on the night train, spend the day there and catch the night train back again. That's what I always do. Saves no end of time, isn't it?' Dazed, I thanked him very much.

In Glasgow for the day (first-class sleeper both ways) I liked the look of Ian, much quieter than his brother, modest and slow to speak. 'Never had an assistant before; been thinking about it for years. If you decide to come, better to play yourself in. No great rush.'

Ian took me to meet his cousin Will, the largest single shareholder and expert on printing and binding. My interview with him was brief and frosty. He asked me what I knew about running a business.

'Nothing at all, I'm afraid.'

'Nothing? But you must know *something*, surely?'

'No, really nothing.'

'I suppose you *might* learn . . .'

I was somewhat taken aback by his hostility but it was no good my pretending to be ideal 'management' material so I said as little as possible. I thought that I was probably just an excuse for a round of cousinly in-fighting. I learned later that these rows were commonplace and that Billy and Ian combined always won them. But Will had a point and the business of management as well as the management of business was becoming fashionable.

Even after 30 years at Macmillan, 20 of them as a director and Managing Director of the General Books Company with a seat on the Holdings Company board, I never learned how to run a business. Billy Collins was a successful tycoon in publishing and he (and others like him) would tell you that 'management' is bunk and that understanding your trade and doing the right thing, not theorising about it, is what matters. Comforting enough for the likes of me, but people like Billy weren't fazed by numbers and the mere sight of a balance sheet didn't make them roll their eyes and slink off to the pub.

Before I left for London Ian offered me the job and I accepted it.

Glasgow was the birthplace of Collins when in 1819 the first Mr William Collins set up a printing press there. The separate London establishment for publishing new general books was started by Sir Godfrey Collins nearly 100 years later and the list grew and prospered throughout the inter-war years.

In 1951 the Glasgow business was also thriving and it was there that all Collins books were printed, bound, invoiced and despatched. It was also where bibles and prayer-books, Collins Classics, Ready Reckoners, school books and rewards (school prizes), ledgers leather-bound with marbled edges, children's annuals and picture-books, diaries and birthday books were devised, commissioned, edited and published. There was a separate department devoted to the production and scheduling of all the London books for Chairman Billy and his band of glamorous layabouts lolling in their editorial armchairs in St James's Place. There was no love lost between Glasgow and London.

Ian lived on his farm outside the city and drove to work every day; he was reputed to read *The Times* at the wheel on the way. He was a Wimbledon and Davis Cup tennis player and rode in point-to-points in the 1930s. He'd had 'a good war' working with the French Resistance and had been much decorated (Légion d'Honneur, two Croix de Guerre and an OBE) and was generally liked and respected. He proposed me for membership of the Western Club and I noted that on the proposal form he described my occupation as 'Publisher', which I took as an encouraging sign.

As a start to the process of 'playing myself in' Ian devised a six-month crash course in publishing and printing, which meant that I would spend three or four weeks in each of the main publishing departments as well as the printing and binding works. That way I'd get to know people and they'd get used to having me around. He and I would meet from time to time to see how things were going. He took endless trouble over these arrangements and I was for some time blinded to the fact that he'd never had an assistant before because he didn't need one.

I began my training, lurking in managers' offices, getting in the way of cheerfully blasphemous printers, weighing small scraps of paper in the paper-buyer's cubby-hole and writing blurbs for a series of picture books about Robin Hood. I even had a spell in the Accounts Department where I was allowed to add up (wrongly the first time) the monthly expenses of the London editors. I particularly enjoyed a month in the printing works partly because Joe Garrigan, the manager, was amused by and sympathetic to my situation. When one of his assistants went on holiday he told me to take over his work. This was to keep all the mighty presses rolling by devising separate programmes for each machine and then switching them every day to cater for changes in priorities and other emergencies. Of course I couldn't have done it on my own and Joe took all the decisions, but having something useful to do was very good for my morale. Joe and I became friends and kept in touch for years after I'd left.

I was really a highly privileged apprentice with a key to the managers' lavatories and lunching rights in the managers' canteen which I sensibly did not exercise. Although I look back fondly to Glasgow I never felt that I belonged to it, even on a Saturday night.

I found a large bed-sitting room in a tenement block near the Botanical Gardens and was lucky in my landlady and her husband. If I wasn't going out she gave me high tea at 6.45; an amicable compromise between six o'clock (her choice) and half-past seven (mine), and I listened to *The Archers* while I had my fry-up. At eight o'clock sharp we played three-handed solo washed down with a bottle of Empire hock in front of my coal fire. They didn't mind my occasional visitors from the South sleeping on the sofa, for which the charge was minimal. When I took the room I didn't say anything about Donald. Maclean is a very common name in the west of Scotland. But my mother rang up one evening when I was out which was a great success with both parties and I suspect that my mother gave Mrs Highet a résumé of my entire life. Anyway I knew the cat was out of the bag the next day when she asked me about my 'other' brother. From then on our relationship blossomed into friendship and she monitored all my incoming calls and enjoyed playing the dragon.

On Wednesday evenings I usually went to the Glasgow White City Greyhound Stadium with Ronald Mongredien, the king of the Collins Ready Reckoner editors. In those pre-calculator days all the figures were done by hand and Ronald's passion for numbers led him to evolve an extremely complicated and interesting betting system based on longest losing sequences of Individual Trap Numbers in each race which demanded hours of laborious calculations each week. Sometimes it worked with staggering success; our most dramatic win was when the system indicated that the dog in Trap 3 should win and the dog in Trap 5 should be second in the fourth race. The two animals concerned were the rank outsiders and looked the part. No one gave them a chance. But Ronald's was a numbers system and we stuck to it. Running true to form our two dogs were lolloping miserably way behind the other four until the final bend where an almighty dog fight erupted among the leaders who disappeared into the crowd. Our dogs were too far behind to be concerned, or even aware of this alternative attraction, and ambled to the winning line alone. The Tote paid nearly £50 to a two-shilling stake on the forecast and Ronald and I threw our hats in the air. But like all systems you had to keep faith with it when it struck a bad patch. Our stakes were low because our pay was low (and Ronald had a family to feed) but we kept afloat in the wilderness weeks and we won a good deal more than we lost over the months of our partnership. Whenever we brought off a coup, however modest, we would invade the whisky-laden gloom of the old Western Club and celebrate quietly like exultant mice.

The Collinses governed their business on strictly feudal lines and the hierarchy from the family downwards was not to be mucked about with. I didn't fit in credibly with any particular stratum of the Collins pyramid and if I innocently crossed lines nobody seemed to mind. Nearly everyone was aware that I was Donald's brother but the only time anyone mentioned it was when the operator of an enormous printing machine churning out vast sheets of pages of the Bible beckoned me over. All he wanted to say, above the din, was that I didn't look anything like the newspaper photographs of Donald. 'Oh, don't I?' I said feebly 'No, you don't and more's the pity!' he said and roared with laughter.

The only occasion when differences in rank were temporarily abandoned and we were encouraged to be one big happy family was on the annual summer outing 'doon the watter' on a Clyde-side steamer. Beer, tea, sausage rolls and cakes were available on board but many groups brought their own whisky. The steamer stopped at one point to pick up the family which included Ian's and Billy's old mother. She'd been attending this ritual jaunt for many years and must have known literally hundreds of the staff. A chat with her was much prized and her royal progress round the boat was marvellous to behold. On this, my first and only outing, I was asked to take a dram with far too many groups and I have only the haziest recollection of getting home. But it was all very friendly.

Billy was the Chairman of the whole firm and was usually present at the outing on the Clyde. Otherwise he came to Glasgow for Board meetings and crises only. He wasn't interested in our affairs unless they affected the production and distribution of the General Books list. Glasgow's scorn for the old enemy in St James's Place was tempered by fear and on his brief appearances you could almost smell it in the air. There were very occasional symptoms of rebellion and one of my happiest recollections is of getting to work at 8.30 one morning when Billy and his wife Pierre (a recent convert to Rome) were expected off the night train from Euston. I found a platoon of men and women frantically scrubbing the walls on either side of the main entrance. The legend, created in huge capital letters in brown paint, read FUCK THE POPE. The scrubbers won their race against the clock and Billy never got the message. Management breathed again.

In the summer of 1952 Ian and I abandoned the pretence that I was ever going to assist him. Mark Bonham Carter had, unbeknownst to me, been working on Billy to get me 'closer to the centre of things' and it was agreed that I should transfer to St James's Place and work as No. 2 to the Publicity Manager Ronald Politzer, then and until his death the best book publicist in London. This seemed to suit everyone except poor Ronald who thought it was a rotten plan.

Saying goodbye to my Glasgow friends was a wrench and I was just getting interested in the Time and Motion antics of the team of Business Consultants who were hovering in the printing and binding workshops and in the warehouse, their stop-watches at the ready. They were objects of suspicion and amusement and the unions were tooling up for battle. I never found out what happened except that after a decent interval the stop-watchers folded their tents and departed. No blood was spilled.

I set off with a light heart on the final stage of my re-education for a month 'on the road' as bag-carrier to the Collins salesman in the North Midlands. His job was to subscribe new general books and to stock up booksellers with standard back-list titles. We were based in Birmingham and roved around towns and cities in neighbouring counties. This included a few days in Nottingham and Wolverhampton where we were joined by Ian Chapman, then No. 3 in the Bible Department and soon to begin his meteoric rise through the ranks. Ian had been selling Collins Bibles in America for most of the time I was in Glasgow, so we didn't know each other well. But our week together, he flogging the Word and Mr Hutchings and I spreading the Flesh and the Devil, created a bond which lasts to this day. In fact Collins didn't go in for Flesh much at that time but I'd already had a glimpse of things to come when I'd discovered a friend, an un-privileged trainee, hunched over a copy of a large American novel. He was making short, stabbing marks with his pen on every page. I watched him for a bit and then asked him what he was doing. He had a slight stammer and explained proudly that he was 't-taking the f-fucks out of *F-from here to Eternity*.'

As I left Glasgow I had the grace to be thankful for many things and grateful to many people. If they were appalled by me or sorry for me they never let me see it. Glaswegians have warm hearts and stunningly good manners.

When you walked into the St James's Place office you could tell at once whether Billy was on the premises or not. He had an electric presence uncomfortable in its force. He laughed a lot but I never thought he was really amused and certainly he had no sense of the ridiculous. He was a man of contradictory qualities – boyish and ruthless, athletic but clumsy in movement as if the room he happened to be in was too small for him, naif yet overpowering. He talked all the time, interspersing his monologues with 'Isn't it?'s which first confused and then hypnotised his hearers. He never appeared to listen to anyone else so conversations of a rational nature were not to be had with him. I became mesmerised to such an extent by the 'Isn't it's' that, while waiting for the next one, I sometimes missed altogether the point of what he was saying. And there always was a point lurking sharp-toothed under the verbiage.

But as a publisher he was formidable, shrewd, able to call on the literary advice he sometimes needed to back up his instinctive judgments of books and authors, an aggressive manipulator and a relentless driver of his staff. During my short stay most of the advice came from Mark and, behind the scenes, from Pierre. Milton Waldman, his chief adviser for several years, had moved to Rupert Hart-Davis and the other editors (among whom were my ex-Glasgow friend Robin Denniston and a new friend George Hardinge) were people he trusted only to a limited extent. They were there to be harried, teased, overborne and incorporated in his natural scheme of things – based on the simple premise that you get the best out of people if you keep them both guessing and at each others' throats.

Above all he was a magnificent salesman expecting, and sometimes getting, the all but impossible from his employees, booksellers, reviewers and literary editors – indeed anyone who could possibly further the cause of selling more Collins books. By that he meant, of course, the books he published and not the Glasgow rubbish. Such commitment to marketing could not be ignored by literary agents and their authors. He had the best Sales Director (Goldsack) and the best Publicity Manager (Politzer) in the country and he knew to an inch what they were capable of and how far he could go in the constant warfare he waged against them. The salesmen knew that he knew the capabilities and capacities of all their major customers as well as they did and they trembled when he looked at their orders, which he did every day.

Billy was not fortunate in his choice of me as No. 2 to Politzer, who wanted, reasonably enough, someone with experience of promoting book sales. It took me ages to realise that my appointment had been made solely to annoy Ronald – so in that sense it was a howling success – and once I'd discovered that, I felt better about my failure to give my immediate boss either pleasure or satisfaction. It seemed to me that a lot of our advertising copy was boring and self-important and Ronald told me tartly to draft some copy for the show-card to accompany booksellers' window displays of stuffed birds and books. The book was *The Field Guide to the Birds of Britain and Europe*. A popular song of that time was called 'How much is that doggie in the window?' and I adapted it:

How much is that Birdie in the window?
The one with the waggley tail?

Won't you please step inside
And inspect the Field Guide
It's the books not the birds is for sale

Ronald was quite huffy about it and said it was both frivolous and ungrammatical. 'That was my intention,' I said grandly. 'Well it's not mine.' So I gave up on the copy-writing revolution.

But Billy hadn't done with Ronald and me. There was more mileage and more fun to be had. Ronald went away for a fortnight's holiday in the spring of 1953, so I was temporarily in charge of the department. He had left me explicit and detailed instructions on just about everything 'and for God's sake no puerile jokes in the advertising'. I was nervous but all went well enough, even in my direct dealings with Billy and Goldsack, who had eyed me with concentrated loathing from our first meeting. To my astonishment, Billy professed himself delighted with my performance. How could Politzer have so wantonly underrated me? Perhaps he was so concerned with his own status that he couldn't recognise a blazing talent for publicity when it was stuck (by Billy) in front of his very nose? He would reorganise the Publicity Department at once. Bonham-Carter had been right about Maclean all along.

So when Ronald returned he found that I had been given half his job as an independent command. In future he was to devote himself full-time to long-range publicity campaigns for individual books and continue to be accountable for the department's budget. I could look after the rest. After all, he'd always complained of being overworked, isn't it? I was appalled and bemused. Ronald was neither. He knew exactly what had happened and it says a lot for him that he didn't blame me or accuse me of treachery. He accepted it, at least outwardly, with extreme calm and he wasn't going to give Billy the satisfaction of seeing him annoyed or in any way put out.

But from then on he became quite human, even friendly, towards me, abandoning his role of Olympian, contemptuous master and we became allies, for better or for worse, in the daily skirmishes with our employer. We both knew that Billy's enthusiasm for me couldn't last for more than a few months at most but we contrived to keep our united front intact until I left for the sylvan glades of Macmillan nearly a year later.

Ronald's promotions went from strength to strength. He had just completed a triumphant campaign for General Montgomery's memoirs when we met for lunch in 1959 and I said it was ridiculous that he hadn't been made a director long ago. Why didn't he just tell Billy that he wanted a seat on the Board? He was shocked. 'My dear Alan! You have to be *elected*.'

Ronald was finally 'elected' after Joy Adamson's book about her lioness *Born Free* swept all before it in 1960, but sadly he died of cancer well before reaching pensionable age (George Hardinge maintained that this was mandatory for all highly paid Collins employees). At his memorial service Billy gave the Address, successfully combining business with obsequies by listing every Collins bestseller since the war.

When I resigned I think everyone was relieved but too polite to say so. Billy asked me if my mind was absolutely made up, Ian wrote me a charming letter from Glasgow, Ronald wished me luck and 'God knows who I'll get lumbered with this time,' and Goldsack told me that he'd never heard of such base ingratitude and in any case why was I going to a dump like Macmillan's? My friends were pleased for me, though nervous that a change of context might provoke a tidal wave of alcohol which would finally sweep me across the Styx. Their fears were nearly realised, but not quite.

In 1962 there was a strong bid from America for Pan (the leading paperback house after Penguin) owned by a consortium of London publishers. Two of them – Macmillan and Collins – exercised their right to match the bid and buy the company.

Billy and Ian Collins and Ian Chapman were the Collins directors and Maurice Macmillan, Rache Lovat Dickson and I represented Macmillan. I hadn't seen Ian since I'd left Glasgow ten years earlier but both he and Billy greeted me warmly at the first meeting of the new Board. I asked Ian if he'd got an assistant at last and he smiled and shook his head. 'I'm still thinking about it.' Billy said, 'It's funny how things can turn out for the best if you give them the chance, isn't it?' Maurice said, 'Speak for yourselves.'

I let that ride; it was a good moment for me.

10. *Mr Dan & Co*

By the beginning of 1954 I knew that if I was to find an agreeable niche in publishing it would have to be as an editor. I hadn't got further than hoping that something would turn up when my (and Donald's) friends Lees and Mary Mayall asked me to stay for the weekend in Paris where Lees was working in the British Embassy.

They had quite a large lunch party and I found myself sitting next to Nancy Mitford which was fine except that I was fuddled enough to think that she was Monica Dickens. I told her how much I'd enjoyed *One Pair of Hands* and when she responded only coolly to that, I said that I'd admired *One Pair of Feet* even more. She neither spoke to nor looked at me again and I suppose she thought I was trying to bait her. I realised of course that I'd offended her but I couldn't think how or why.

I was telling my troubles to a friendly, sympathetic woman after lunch and when she had stopped laughing she solved the mystery for me. There was absolutely nothing to be done about it. And then I saw across the room a tall dark-haired man weaving drunkenly between book-case and door. He was good-looking in a smashed sort of way. I said 'Who's that broken-down Heathcliff?'

'Maurice Macmillan,' she said and added 'My husband. Somehow this doesn't seem to be your day. Never mind, come and meet him. Mary, my sister, says you're a publisher now. Maurice longs not to be a publisher but he's rather stuck in the family business.'

Maurice and I had an agreeable hour chatting and weaving before I left to catch my plane back to London. I resolved not to speak to strangers on the way.

After our first meeting in Paris Maurice and I saw quite a lot of each other and it was while I was staying with him and Katie in Sussex that he asked me if I would like to consider joining Macmillan. He was quite vague about the job and said, 'We need someone to help Rache Lovat Dickson with the general books. But of course we don't want someone who would be too grand to edit a German grammar or two.' I said I wasn't too grand but too ignorant. Maurice was surprised and slightly aggrieved 'Could have sworn you said you spoke German. Oh well, it's the not-being-too-grand bit that really matters.'

'I can do that all right.'

Maurice said that was fine then and he'd talk to his uncle, and get me in to meet him. The real point for him, Maurice, was that he wanted to make his life in politics not publishing. Before very long, he said, he would have to succeed his uncle as chairman and he wanted to import a few friends who could eventually help run the firm while he got on with the politics. He might as well start with me now as I was able and willing and had a few years experience elsewhere under my belt.

It all sounded too good to be true and, as the weeks went by, I feared that that was just what it was.

However one evening Maurice rang up and invited me to lunch at the Macmillan office the next day. I dug out my cleanest shirt and managed to slink off early from Collins to have a calming drink on my way. It was a stately 'purpose-built' edifice in St Martin's Street, the lane running between Leicester and Trafalgar Squares, and the dark oak-panelled entrance hall was large and silent. The elderly gentleman, Mr Gray, whose domain it was, gave me a courteous welcome. When Maurice appeared and led me up the grand staircase he mentioned that Mr Gray always showed his poetry to Osbert Sitwell in draft and never typed it until it had been blessed by Osbert's approval. I was impressed. We made our way through a rabbit warren of offices, some with clerks crouched on high stools at tall ledger desks, and into a snug little dining-room where Daniel Macmillan and Rache (short for Horatio) Lovat Dickson, the editorial director, were waiting.

Mr Macmillan was a slim, slight, elderly man with white hair, a pale face and ferocious eyebrows. Everything about him was quick – mind, movement, speech, temper and wit. He wore half-glasses on the end of his nose and his almond-shaped hooded eyes could switch from twinkle to glare and back again with alarming speed. Addicted to dark blue suits and black shoes he was always in a hurry and preferred running to walking in the corridors and passages of St Martin's Street. He lunched nearly every day with the same old cronies at the same corner table at the Garrick Club.

A Balliol scholar he took a Double First at Oxford and joined the family firm in 1910. Invalided out of the Army in 1915 he returned to the office and it remained his life until shortly before his death in 1965. In 1936 the three old Macmillan partners, including his father, died within six months of each other. He became Chairman and with his younger (by eight years) brother Harold joint Managing Director. They remained close friends for the rest of his life. Although Harold's political career took him away from the business for long periods the two brothers were never out of touch and Harold's affection for Dan was tinged with something like reverence. Both were prone to occasional fits of black depression and Dan's moods were never less than variable.

That day, fortunately for me, his mood was positively sunny. He had spent the morning at an interesting, if profitless, meeting of Robert Maxwell's creditors and he told us the latest about 'that Maxwell fellow' and the collapse of Simpkin Marshall, the book-wholesale house which Maxwell had bought and bankrupted, leaving many publishers, including Macmillan, with large accounts unpaid. 'What a crook!' he said, but he sounded half-admiring.

Lovat Dickson was polite but distant and as we made the most of our lunch he said very little. Nobody said anything about a job.

After lunch Dan got up abruptly, asked me to follow him and hurried out of the room. I had to run to catch up with him and would certainly have lost my way if I hadn't.

When we reached his lair at the end of the long directors' corridor which stretched across the width of the original building, he gave me a chair and sat at his enormous desk.

'Maurice tells me that you want to join us?'

'Yes, sir, I'd like that very much.'

'Well, I always think that first impressions are best, so if you want to come you'd better come. You can give Rache a hand with the General List. We'll pay you whatever Collins give you. When can you come?'

'I suppose I should give a month's notice, if that would be all right?'

'Good,' he looked at his diary, 'in fact splendid. Come on April 1st. That's a good day to start.'

He seemed almost as pleased as I was and I found that rather puzzling. It was exciting for me but surely no reason for what almost looked like glee on his part. However I thought no more about it in my great elation.

The reason for his glee did not emerge for nearly 20 years (long after he and Rache had retired). I was talking to Howard Clewes, who had recently returned from America after a long stint of script-writing in Hollywood. He had published a couple of novels with Macmillan in the early 1950s and we had just accepted his latest. He and I had not met before and I saw that he was looking at me quizzically. Suddenly he said,

'Do you realise you've got my job?'

'Good heavens! No. How?'

'Well, in 1954 Rache kept pressing me to join Macmillan to work with him and eventually, because I couldn't seem to get started on another novel and funds were low, I said I would. About a week later he rang me up to say it was all off because he'd had some young man foisted on him by the Macmillans themselves and there wasn't a damn thing he could do about it. They hadn't even consulted him.'

'God. How awful. I *am* sorry.'

'Not your fault. And anyway it's probably worked out better for both of us this way.'

It must have slowly dawned on Rache during that lunch that he'd been rail-roaded and quite naturally he became huffier by the minute. He and Dan were very old friends and if their friendship had become a bit frayed at the edges one can see why. Dan loved baiting people, friend and foe alike, and this was an opportunity for an enormous Rache-tease. The unkindness was sharpened rather than softened by making my appointment to be effective on All Fools Day.

The first day of any new job has a charm all its own in that nothing that has gone before can possibly be your fault. You are in all things blissfully beyond reproach. Blank pieces of paper, empty In-tray, virgin blotting-paper and a silent telephone are your symbols of high endeavour to come.

I arrived much too early (about 9 a.m.) and was escorted by the affable poet, Mr Gray, to what was to be my office for the next ten years. Maurice had been the previous occupant and he had now removed next door to his father's old office. Mr Gray gravely intimated that it might be an hour or so before the big-shots turned up for another week at the coal-face. He left me with civil good wishes.

My oak-panelled nest was quite large boasting an expanse of shining parquet floor, a long table, a 'partners' desk (seats two) and a hideously uncomfortable but elegant wicker-work upright chair with mahogany arms for visitors. I was thankful that Maurice had left me an ash-tray.

After a bit I summoned up the courage to go for a cautious prowl along the directors' corridor. After the edgy rough and tumble of Collins the House of Macmillan seemed like a haven of prosperous peace and quiet. A Victorian air of respectability had not faded with the passing years and the portraits of 19th-century divines which graced the panelling on one side of the corridor retained their authority. They were all early Macmillan authors and included Charles Kingsley, Archdeacon Hare and F. D. Maurice, but I couldn't put a name to any one of them. They were a stern lot and, like most fashionable portraits of the day, their eyes followed one with cool disapproving stares. I had to pass them to get to my office every day and sometimes, as I brought my hangover late to work, I couldn't face them and scuttled past with my head averted.

My first visitor was a cheerful girl who put her head round the door and offered to bring me a cup of coffee. When I accepted she hesitated and said, 'Forgive me for asking, but are you a director?'

'No, I'm not. Does that rule out the coffee?'

'Gosh no! It's just that we're short of cups and saucers. I don't suppose you'll mind having a mug?'

'Heavens no!'

'Oh good! We'd all die without coffee.'

The dregs of my coffee were still warm when my door was opened abruptly and Mr Dan appeared, accompanied by a large clean-cut man wearing a smart grey suit and an Old Rugbeian tie. He was pink of face and was clearly both cross and embarrassed. Mr Dan wasted no time.

'Now have you got everything you need? Pens, pencils, paper, paper-clips, ink, india-rubber?'

'Yes, I'm fine, thank you, sir.'

'Well, anything you want just tell Clark here and he'll get it for you. Also,' he said, looking at the parquet floor as if for the first time, 'what about a carpet?'

'I'm perfectly happy without one.'

'But would you *like* one?'

'Well, um . . .'

'Now look here,' he said 'we haven't got all day – do you or do you not want a carpet? Yes or no?'

'Yes, please.'

'Good, that's settled then. Go to Harvey Nichols this afternoon and buy one. Tell them to send the bill to Clark.'

He was gone as suddenly as he had appeared, leaving Clark and me to pick up our lives as best we could.

'Is he always like that?'

'Yes and no. He can be worse.'

'Did he really mean that about the carpet?'

'Yes, he did. You're quite honoured, you know. A new carpet and all those paper-clips isn't a bad haul for your first day. I hope you'll live up to them.' He smiled for the first time. 'My name's Bob Rowland Clark. I'm the Company Secretary and the Finance Director but you'll find that titles don't mean a great deal here. Mr Dan doesn't like any of us to get too big for our boots – as you'll have noticed.'

'I'm a good scrounger when it comes to things like paper-clips.'

'I hoped you might be. Anyway, good luck.'

So my first (and only guilt-free) day ended in the carpet department at Harvey Nichols. When I saw Maurice the next morning he said he'd been looking for me the day before. Perhaps I'd got lost? 'No,' I said, 'your uncle told me to go and buy a carpet, so that's what I did.'

'Ah,' he said, 'that accounts for it. When I saw him he was extra-pleased with himself but only said, "I do hope *your* friend doesn't expect anyone to tell him what to do."'

Like other feudal family firms, including Collins, the active Macmillan family partners were known by their Christian names with a Mister stuck in front. So we had Misters Dan and Maurice, Mister Arthur (our occasional consultant on religious books) and Mister Harold (absent for political reasons). Non-family directors and the next layer or two down below the Board were known by their initials with a Mr, Mrs or even Miss prefix as required. I didn't at all mind becoming Mr ADM and the arrangement conferred a certain dignity on all of us blessed in this way. Of course this mister business also implied amateur status (like 'gentlemen' jockeys) which was a bit unfortunate in that we were meant to be competing with other publishing houses who were unashamedly professional.

As far as General Books were concerned we were still living off the fat of past generations. Our back list included such money-spinning giants as Hardy, Kipling, Yeats, Henry James, Lewis Carroll and Frazer's *Golden Bough; Gone With the Wind* (published in 1939) was still booming away in hard-cover at the full price. But when I arrived new novels by Rebecca West, Charles Morgan and Mazo de la Roche were about to be published and the first printings of 30,000 copies apiece were soon sold without any noticeable promotion or effort. So it was not surprising that Mr Dan saw no reason to go in for such new-fangled vulgarities as sales and marketing departments. The publicity department was not encouraged to do much more than advertisements in the Sunday newspapers and the *TLS*, to produce catalogues and the spring and autumn lists for new books.

Macmillan had four full-time representatives (salesmen), one of whom called on all the central London accounts while the other three covered the rest of the British Isles. They all wore hats. The three 'sales' departments – Town, Country and Overseas – were there to process orders not to solicit them.

It's true that Charles Morgan always doubled the advertising budget for his new novels out of his own pocket and if he had not been an exceptionally kind man my brilliant career might have come to a sticky end almost before it had started. Rache had asked me to take a look at the copy for a solus advertisement in the *Observer* for Charles' new (and last as it happened) novel *Challenge to Venus* and I thought it was a bit dull. The reviews had been good and it was selling out of the shops in bucketloads but there was no room for a lot of quotes so I suggested that we should just say something to the effect that for once a really good novel was getting its deserved rewards of excellent sales and excellent reviews. I roughed out a draft which the publicity department accepted but there was no time for a proof. What appeared is reproduced opposite, and luckily Charles thought it was funny.

When I apologised he said that he'd always wondered what it would be like to be shot in the back by his own men. This was a relatively painless way of finding out. There were no recriminations but it gave Mr Dan the opportunity to say to Maurice that he was glad to see that I didn't seem to expect anyone to tell me what not to do either.

Mr Dan's secret weapon for keeping control of events was, Maurice told me, his 'cards' which he kept locked up in an enormous filing cabinet in his office. Nobody else had ever set eyes on them but they were believed to record in his own handwriting the life history of every book on any of the various Macmillan lists. He came into the deserted office every Saturday morning to bring them up-to-date. He made no secret of the existence of the cards but they were a part of his private life which he guarded closely. Perhaps his obsession with privacy dated back to his early days in the firm when he had the reputation of being a Stage-door Johnny by night as well as a Macmillan director by day, which earned him the disapproval of his father and two uncles. Family mythology also credited him with a habit of giving away shares in the business to chorus-girls after particularly enjoyable nights on the tiles. This meant that the Macmillan family lawyer had to go round the next day and buy them back. I've always longed to believe this.

Mr Dan was a genuine eccentric in that he had no idea that he was anything of the sort and his frequent explosions were as short-lived as they were colourful. He wrote many of his letters in his own hand and did some of his own filing. Although this made it difficult for his secretary to assist him in a conventional way the three successive women who worked for him in the years I knew him all found him endlessly surprising and entertaining. He took up rather less than a third of their time so they were able to pursue simultaneously other careers within the firm. Two of them became excellent editors and the third and last of the three developed a flair for selling foreign language and other subsidiary rights and was later to be one of the first women to be made a director of a Macmillan company. They were all formidable, highly intelligent persons with senses of humour to match.

Going back a bit further, the Macmillans continued to employ men as secretaries long after this role had become almost exclusively female elsewhere. There was still one in place in the 1950s, but the best-known was Mr Dan's former secretary/sparring partner, Mr Geekie, whose eccentricity matched that of his boss. Mr Dan was attached to him because he gave as good as he got and was a master of that most sophisticated of Army 'crimes' – Dumb Insolence. When Mr Geekie overstepped some invisible line of insubordination, dumb or otherwise, Mr Dan hurled books at him. The book-throwing episodes invariably ended in an apology from master to man which was loftily accepted. I met the old gentleman once at the Annual Christmas Dinner for staff and pensioners at Lyons Corner House in Piccadilly. He told me that he was 'a bit wobbly on my pins' but his bright blue eyes gave due warning that he still had all his marbles. He wore a smart black jacket, pin-striped trousers, white shirt, black tie and stiff winged collar (his customary attire in his working days). I felt that we might have something in common in that he had shared what was now my office with Mr Harold's (lady) secretary in the 1930s. I also knew that the sharing had not been a success because he liked to cook kippers on a paraffin stove at lunch-time which made the place pretty well uninhabitable in the afternoons. However, he clearly did not think that this constituted any sort of bond between us and he moved on as soon as he decently could. Still, I was glad to have spoken to a legend.

Knowing now how little my appointment can have pleased him, I'm amazed by Rache Lovat Dickson's friendliness towards me from the start. He was tall, handsome, immaculately dressed and groomed with grey hair brushed into wings at the temples and he looked every inch a successful publisher. He still had a vestige of a Canadian accent from his youth and there was about him a faint aura of expensive after-shave lotion.

In 1928 Rache had been about to take up a teaching job at the University of Alberta when a Canadian millionaire who had just bought *The Fortnightly Review* in London acted on a fairy-godmotherish whim and sent him across the Atlantic to be its assistant editor. Within four years he had founded his own publishing house and a literary magazine, both bearing his name.

He had his share of instant success when he received through the post the typescript of *Pilgrims of the Wild* by Grey Owl, an Ojibway Indian half-breed from the Canadian backwoods. It was an immediate best-seller and the two frantic lecture tours which Rache organised in 1935 and 1937 not only boosted sales but also culminated in a Command Performance at Buckingham Palace for the King and Queen and the two young princesses. Keeping Grey Owl reasonably sober and persuading him to sleep in his own bed was a full-time job and the Red Indian's sudden death on his return to Saskatchewan came as no great surprise. The surprise was provided by the press, who discovered that Grey Owl's real name was Archie Belaney and that he had spent the first 15 years of his life in the Sussex seaside town of Hastings in the care of his two maiden aunts.

Despite this enormous windfall, or rather because of it, the firm was expanding without enough capital to finance it. Sadly, Rache sold out to another small publisher, Peter Davies, and, as World War II approached, he accepted his friend Dan Macmillan's invitation to join his firm. He worked as No. 2 to Harold Macmillan on General Books until the latter was given office by Churchill when he succeeded Chamberlain as Prime Minister in 1940. Rache then took over as Editorial Director.

Of course he gained much by giving up his independence in favour of the financial security ('wife and child to support') and prestige available to him at Macmillan, but it wasn't nearly as much fun. He had some notable successes over the years including Richard Hillary's *The Last Enemy*, which was a massive war-time best seller and is still going strong over 50 years later, but I think that he longed for the freedom, the hazards and the sheer excitement of being his own boss and running his own small firm, for better or for worse.

To go and work for a friend, whatever the advantages, puts dangerous pressures on both parties to the friendship. And when the friend is both the owner of the business and an irascible old tyrant with a taste and a talent for mockery and human bear-baiting, the fun becomes too one-sided for comfort. The gradual loss of confidence in each other's judgment and the ebbing of the mutual respect which went with it must have been painful for Rache, though I doubt that it was more than another source of irritation to Mr Dan. The practical joke of employing me without consulting Rache was a fair example of how far their relationship had deteriorated. But Rache was possessed of great tenacity, courage and optimism and these qualities combined with his long friendships with many of his authors served to keep him cheerfully afloat.

In any event he must have decided to make the best of a bad job and took me out to lunch with Osbert Sitwell on my second day and with Charles Morgan the day after. It was rather like a racehorse trainer introducing the new stable-boy to two of his string's most venerable stars – easy to ride, good manners, no bucking and squealing when taken out of their boxes, and don't try to bite you when you feed them. He gave me a few typescripts to read and report on and also a proof copy of a book which was already in production called *Pre-stressed Concrete* by an eminent scientist, Dr Kurt Billig. He said he was sure that I would soon bring in new authors of my own but that I might like to have one ready-made (like the concrete as it were) to cut my Macmillan teeth on. 'Just drop him a line and say how pleased you are to be looking after him and his book and so on.' Dr Billig and I conducted a friendly, if formal, correspondence and publication duly took place without a hitch, no thanks to me. I've always felt grateful to him for being 'my' first author and in later years when asked who were Macmillan's main authors at that time I would slip in his name between Enid Blyton and A.L. Rowse just for luck.

Mr Dan's chief publishing concern had always been the Educational lists and he still kept them on a tight rein. The General List had been Harold's pigeon but the two brothers had followed the practice of the two preceding generations and shared the responsibility for every book published under their imprint.

When Rache succeeded Harold as Editorial Director of the General List he did not inherit any other of the latter's responsibilities and every new book had to receive Mr Dan's blessing, or at least his assent, before it was accepted. He also fixed the price and printing number and personally approved the design, paper and binding of each book. Our

Production Manager H. A. Evans, a sardonically difficult man, was extremely good at his job and took orders only from Mr Dan, who paid him four or five visits a day. We could in fact communicate with each other by telephone but only through the good offices of our operator who shared Mr Dan's view that the telephone should only be used as a last resort. Barking down it was a poor substitute for barking in person. Hence all the flying visits.

I realised very early on that if I wanted to have a say in what a particular book looked like I would have to nobble Mr Evans before the design process got under way. He disliked attempted interference by editors, all of whom (including Rache) he regarded as boobies. However, he was old-fashioned enough to read a lot and if he liked a book he would take great trouble over it and I gradually got to know and to like him. I no longer got his stock response to editorial whingeing: 'Don't ask me, go and tell Mr Dan what you want.' One day I got up the courage to ask him what his Christian name was. 'I'm not going to tell you,' he said. 'You'll have to guess.' 'Horace?' I ventured. 'That'll do,' he replied, 'for both of us.' From then on we called each other Horace.

Simona Pakenham had published a biography of Vaughan Williams with Macmillan a year or two before I arrived and Horace not only admired her writing but also liked her. He told me that she was writing another book about the colony of English painters and writers who had settled at Dieppe in the early years of the century. I suggested that he should persuade her to offer it to us. 'All right,' he said, 'but I don't want her buggered about, mind.' In due course we published this delightful book which she called *Thirty Miles from England*. Needless to say it was most beautifully produced.

Mr Dan held an editorial meeting for the General List every Wednesday at 11 o'clock sharp. It was the arena in which books were accepted or rejected and where we were alleged to have the chance to discuss ideas and make proposals for new books to commission. Of course, in 'arena' terms, we were the Christians and Mr Dan was the lions and we usually came off second best. When this thought first occurred to me I also realised that he closely resembled the lion in Tenniel's drawing of the Lion and the Unicorn in *Alice in Wonderland*.

These Wednesday meetings were particularly hellish for Mr Thomas Mark, the best of editors and by tradition the custodian of all the typescripts and reports from our small band of regular readers. He was a Pickwickian figure a few years younger than Mr Dan, whom he loathed and feared. He told me once in a rare fit of intimacy that because of a family financial crisis he had left school (Rugby) early and had started work at Macmillan as a junior clerk at the age of 17. He had been bitterly disappointed to have missed his University years but his knowledge of and love for English literature survived three years in the trenches during the First World War. On his return to the firm his talents as an editor were slowly recognised; in the early twenties he was made Secretary to the

Above: *Mr Dan with Maurice and self outside Macmillan's St Martin's Street office, and* right: *Tenniel's lion.*

Editorial Board and he worked on the typescripts and proofs of many of Macmillan's famous authors including Hardy, Kipling and Yeats. He was made a director during the Second World War and was now approaching retirement. His memory was phenomenal and his wit caustic, but he had no stomach for the fights which Mr Dan did his best to provoke.

Mr Dan presided at the head of the boardroom table with Maurice at the other end making complicated doodles on a large sheet of white paper. Rache sat on his right and Mr Mark on his left, the week's typescripts and reports in neat piles before him. We were all seated with the door open before running footsteps announced the imminent arrival of the boss. He shut the door with a bang and had already said 'What have we got today?' before reaching his chair.

The trick for getting Mr Dan's approval for a particular book or commission was to make sure it didn't come up for judgment too early in the proceedings. Mr Mark always began with several unfavourable reports so that, like some blood-thirsty mythological dragon devouring the weekly

consignment of virgins, Mr Dan could write a large NO in the margin of the reports and sign his initials below. When he'd turned down four or five no-hopers his mood would change for the better and he might listen to or even ask for our opinions provided they were brief and to some sort of point. But it wasn't altogether as simple as that because he was liable to interrupt Mr Mark's stately reading of reports, telling him to hurry it up, and then to snatch the report from Mr Mark's hand and read it aloud himself in a contemptuous tone of voice. He thus made a fool of Mr Mark, the author of the book and the writer of the report all in one go –

a triple bull's eye.

There was a further booby-trap to be negotiated by those of us hoping to get something 'through', which was his habit of getting suddenly to his feet and running out of the room. Bang went the door. The timing of these disappearances was quite unpredictable but they never lasted for more than a few minutes and when he rushed back he took things up exactly where he'd left them. It was as if he'd switched us all off, very often in someone's mid-sentence, and re-animated us with the magic words, 'Well, go on then.' There were various theories about the cause of these disruptions – a call of nature, a quick drink, consulting his cards, suddenly remembering something he wanted to tell Horace to do? Who knows? My own explanation was (and is) that there would always be a point at any meeting he was at when he simply couldn't bear it a minute longer. His boredom threshold was low.

This happened to me when I was trying to persuade him to re-publish Christopher Burney's *Solitary Confinement*. I'd explained that the original publisher had gone bust on the day of publication in 1952, that it had had rave reviews, had sold out the modest first (and only) impression in a few days and had been in limbo ever since. At this point Mr Dan did a runner, my heart sank and Maurice said, 'That's torn it.' When he came back he glared at me and said irritably, 'Well, go on then.' I asked him if he wanted me to begin at the beginning again. 'Indeed I don't. I'm not deaf. Anyway, who is this man?' peering at my report 'Brunny? *Brunny*? Who's Brunny?'

'His name is Burney and he's now a merchant banker, sir.'

'A merchant *bank*er?' He might just as well have said, 'In a *hand*-bag?' Maurice intervened casually without raising his eyes from his doodle.

'He's a *rich* merchant banker, Uncle Dan.'

Mr Dan allowed himself a broad grin. 'Oh well,' he said. 'In that case tell him we'll publish his book.' Nothing delighted him more than to find a wrong reason for doing a right thing.

He could be relied on to take an interest in any proposal which swam against the run-of-the-mill. He never turned a hair when we proposed to commission a first novel from Muriel Spark. 'Why not? Why not? Tell me that', as though he had made the proposal and we were dragging our sulky feet. The result was *The Comforters*, the beginning of her long brilliant career as a novelist. He was equally sanguine about accepting simultaneously the first seven novels by an unknown middle-aged

Scotswoman living in Jamaica, Jane Duncan. 'I trust she won't just sit back and think that's it.' She wrote another 24 books before she died in 1977.

Books by established Macmillan authors generally went through on the nod and a new offering from Enid Blyton would never, in ordinary circumstances, have found its way on to Mr Mark's pile. But the senior and most powerful of the non-family directors, Roland Heath, had just retired and it was with him that Miss Blyton had dealt exclusively. She used several publishers for her vast output but the *Adventure* series which Mr Heath had acquired for Macmillan (thanks it was said to playing golf with her husband every weekend) was a goldmine rivalled only by *Noddy, The Famous Five* and *The Secret Seven* series which graced the Hodder & Stoughton list. Mr Heath, incidentally, strongly disapproved of Rache and all his works (this included me) and used his position as the Onlie Begetter of the *Adventure* books to snipe at his enemy at board meetings from the moral high ground of high profits.

With Mr Heath gone, Miss Blyton's new book (not one of the *Adventure* series) came in from her agent addressed to the Children's Books editor. This was all right except that we didn't have one. Rache had a few children's authors on his list, including Geoffrey Trease and Rumer Godden whose children's books were as popular as her adult novels, but Enid Blyton was a property apart. Mr Mark started to read out the agent's letter when Mr Dan seized both letter and typescript and, announcing that he would read it himself, bustled out of the room.

The following Wednesday Mr Dan looked like the cat who'd swallowed both the cream and the canary. No one was bullied, everything was sweetness and light and the meeting was over in half the usual time. As he gathered up his papers he said cheerfully that he'd read the Blyton book, thought it was rubbish and wouldn't have it on the list at any price. He handed the typescript to Mr Mark saying, 'Someone had better write to these people and tell them' and off he went. Mr Mark duly wrote one of his best regretful letters and that was that – or would have been but for a small time-bomb ticking away in Bob Rowland Clark's pending tray.

At the time of his retirement Mr Heath had, with Mr Dan's approval, handed over most of his executive responsibilities to Bob and another director and sent each of them a note. At the bottom of Bob's list were the fateful words 'Enid Blyton'. It was several weeks before he got round to the pleasant task of introducing himself, which he did gracefully enough, adding that he hoped it would not be too long before we had something new from her pen. He refused to show me the reply.

Bob was philosophical about the loss of his one ewe lamb and blamed it on the fact that we kept no minutes of our editorial meetings. Rache volunteered to talk to Mr Dan about it but of course it meant telling him about Bob's disastrous letter. He reported that Mr Dan laughed until he cried but was adamant that he wouldn't have minutes. 'We get on perfectly well as we are. No point in shutting a stable door after the mare has fled.' He said, however, that Bob could come to the meetings if he liked. 'Might even learn something about publishing.'

This unfair crack was in revenge for Bob's reasonable, though impassioned, plea at a board meeting that all costings should include a provision for overheads. Costings at that time were done by Mr Maskell, a senior and thrifty member of the Accounts Department, in beautiful handwriting on the backs of used but clean envelopes and Mr Dan incorporated them into his private system for pricing each book so that it would make an acceptable profit if successful. As his system seemed to work quite well for the most part he naturally rejected the idea out of hand and enjoyed himself by making sarcastic references to 'Clark's Overheads' at any meeting he happened to be attending. Anyway Bob accepted this back-handed invitation and said that he would do his best to inject an element of sanity, however small, into our proceedings. Some hope.

The question of minutes came up again after a major rumpus over an American novel which, it seemed, we had published by mistake. It was a good novel which had done well in America and concerned the problems of a bunch of sex-starved 19th-century missionaries in Japan. It had been sent to us along with four or five other American novels recently published there, by a literary agent whose unenviable job it was to try to find British publishers for them. He was I suppose at least going through the motions and felt perhaps that sending books out in an interesting-looking cluster made up for a total lack of information about any of them, except what could be gleaned from the book jackets.

We were nothing if not conscientious about all submissions getting read by somebody and this book fell, or was pushed, into the hands of the poet and critic Sir John Squire who had been reading and reporting on books for his friends the Macmillans for many years. He was by now an old man and his opinions of novels had become polarised; he either gave them an alpha plus or a gamma minus. In this case he had enjoyed the book hugely and wrote his short report accordingly. What none of us could remember was what had happened next nor how it had got on to Mr Mark's 'acceptance' pile. The report had neither a YES or a NO on it but it did have Mr Dan's initials in the margin. Rache had duly signed the contract. The book was printed by photo-litho from the American edition so there were no proofs for anyone to read and the jacket design was adapted for the Macmillan cover. It was priced by Mr Dan himself (*pace* Clark's Overheads) and as publication day approached the first finished copy was placed reverently on his desk. An hour later all hell broke loose.

I was walking sedately down the corridor minding my own business when Mr Dan shot out of his office waving his copy and shouting, 'Who is responsible for this disgusting book?' As I was the only person in sight and already a prime suspect I got the full blast of his wrath. I strongly denied the charge. 'Not I, sir.' Mr Dan gave me a disbelieving glare, turned on his heel and went off to accuse Rache.

It took me back to my kindergarten days when we played a most enjoyably fatuous game in which we all stood in a line except for one child, who faced us and squeaked, 'Who has done this foul deed?' The first in line said, 'Not I, sir,' the child-in-charge said, 'Then who, sir?'

'Number Two, sir.'

'Not I, sir.'

'Then who, sir?'

'Number Three, sir' and so on down the line. The last child named Number One as the guilty party and the whole thing started again, question and answer getting faster and faster until we all collapsed in a heap howling with laughter.

Mr Dan spent the afternoon conducting his inquisition but the evidence (which I have summarised above) was inconclusive and none of the suspects felt up to suggesting that the mere sight of Mr Dan's initials in the margin might have been enough to set the contractual and production wheels turning. Rache and I read the book that night and Mr Dan had calmed down when we reported to him the next morning. He had already come to the conclusion that it was far too late to stop publication without drawing unfavourable notice to ourselves and we should certainly have looked complete idiots if we had tried to. Neither Rache nor I thought it was at all 'disgusting' and even in those unliberated days there could be no danger of offending against the obscenity laws. So we all kept our mouths shut, publication was back on track and the book did rather well.

When Bob courageously resurrected his proposal that minutes should be kept, Mr Dan simply said, 'No, we won't.' But for our own peace of mind Rache and Maurice decreed that we would have a little notebook in which to record decisions. Rex Allen, who was the editor in charge of the Academic Books list and therefore above suspicion when it came to matters of obscenity, gamely offered to keep it unobtrusively. 'Hope I don't get caught,' he said.

Mr Dan, as expected, continued to hold Rache and me responsible for the muddle, if not for deliberately slipping the book into production. He told Mr Mark not to send Jack Squire any more books which might over-excite him and for several weeks pretended to examine carefully any report on an American novel. 'I want to be sure there aren't any more frightful missionaries lurking about.'

But somehow his heart wasn't really in it and I had the uncomfortable feeling that the inner fires which fuelled his head of steam were dying back, and that his pride in being blatantly and often hilariously out of step with the modern world might have been replaced by a depressed suspicion that he was simply out of touch. It was almost a relief to discover that what ailed him was cancer.

After his operation and a long convalescence Mr Dan ignored the advice of his doctors and started to come into the office for a few hours every week to try to get his beloved cards up-to-date. He looked very frail and it seemed most unlikely that he would ever be well enough to take charge of the firm again. Maurice was standing in for him and had to start thinking about what needed to be done if and when his uncle could be persuaded to retire. He was then 75. To this end Maurice wrote a long note to Bob Rowland Clark, setting out the most urgent of the financial reforms which he thought would be necessary. He apparently saw no reason not to send his uncle a copy. The effect was electric and instantaneous – Maurice described it as the quickest cure in medical history. Mr Dan read the note, picked up his hat, stick and coat and as he left his office told his secretary to let everyone know that from then on he would be in the office every day. And so he was.

Our row about the missionaries was a private storm in a private tea-cup but Mr Dan was back in time for the prosecution of Penguin for publishing the unexpurgated version of *Lady Chatterley's Lover*. They did not offer the book for sale to the general public but legally 'published' it by sending a copy to the Director of Public Prosecutions. Their massive defence was already in place beforehand. The trial was long and expensive but Penguin won their acquittal handsomely and conclusively. The final nail in the Prosecution's coffin was hammered in personally by their leader, the Common Sergeant, who, in his final speech to the jury, asked if they could honestly say that they would leave a copy of the book lying about where their servants might see and read it. The 'Not Guilty' verdict caused the obscenity laws to be changed and it also changed the face of the book trade. Authors had no cause to fear the Law and publishers had only to make up their own minds about what they would and would not publish. In our case this meant no change and the final decision would as always be Mr Dan's.

Mr Dan had in fact already moved with the times insofar as he had allowed us to have a real live sales manager for General Books, the number of our salesmen had increased to six and they no longer had to wear hats when calling on their customers. Young faces were appearing on the staff and new writers on the list. But he was unimpressed by the Chatterley verdict – 'Boring book' – and made it quite clear that he wasn't going to have his name on any book which he found offensive. I could see squalls ahead, but in the two remaining years of his chairmanship there was only one row and we lost a good novel, and of course its author, to Eyre & Spottiswode, one of the four publishers licensed to publish the Authorised Version of the Bible. Our legal adviser, who was also a trustee, drily enquired whether this meant that the Holy Bible might have to share a shelf with the offending volume.

Mr Dan seemed no less physically frail in those two years, but in his mind and spirits he was very much himself again. When my mother died in 1962 he asked me how old she was. I hesitated and then said, 'Sad, really, she was only 82.' He thought for a bit. 'I think you're pulling my leg,' and then with a broad smile, 'But thank you all the same.'

When he retired in the spring of 1963 he managed to take us all by surprise. It was as if he was making one of his familiar bolts for the door during a boring meeting, only this time he wasn't coming back. I missed him very much.

11. *Around the World in 99 Cromwell Road*

In a memoir covering the early 1950s a friend described me as having 'a drink problem which he left cheerfully unsolved'. A generous interpretation, I think, but it must have been about that time that I crossed the invisible line separating the heavy drinker from the alcoholic. Most addicts are not aware of their state until some years after they've achieved it. Everyone else knows but they don't. I was no exception and it was not until 1957 that I was ready to admit to myself that I could neither take it nor leave it.

There was no crisis, no drama, no going blind on the road to Damascus. I was sitting in my office at Macmillan labouring over a blurb for a novel, when I decided that I had a problem and that I wanted to solve it. I didn't know how but it was good to have a choice; to be or not to be.

I'd heard of an eccentric, elderly doctor called John Dent who was said to offer a swift chemical treatment with no psychiatric strings. He'd successfully treated the film director, Anthony Asquith, the uncle of Mark Bonham-Carter, who'd been observing my drinking habits with increasing alarm. At least he didn't sound like the pin-striped proprietor of some expensive torture chamber with panoramic views across London from Harrow-on-the-Hill. So I rang him up and got my head bitten off. When I mentioned Asquith's name he shouted that he didn't discuss his patients. Who was I? And what did I want? I said help was what I wanted and that at last seemed to be the right answer.

Dent opened the door in his braces. Short, portly, shaggy white hair and moustaches to match, he wore a Savage Club tie loosely knotted halfway down his front. He looked like an old dog.

'Come in, come in. I'm hoovering the tank.'

He led the way to his sitting-consulting-room at the dark end of which stood a large, brightly lit glass tank, the home of his tropical fish. Guppies, Black Mollies, Tetrons and Neons made respectful rings round a magnificent solitary Siamese Fighting Fish (if you have two they fight) and a large sinister black-scaled Plecostomas, the resident window-cleaner whose enormous round mouth, pressed against the inside of the glass, cleaning it by suction inch by inch. A rubber pipe, one end still in the water, was dripping on to the carpet.

'Hang on a bit till I get this finished. Won't take long. Trick is to get it flowing without getting a mouthful. Have to be below water level.'

He crouched on the floor, sucked on the pipe and as the water began to flow into a bucket, he manipulated the other end like a hoover, sucking up the fish droppings from the gravel floor of the tank. I noticed some of the smaller guppies also disappearing into the pipe line. When he was done, he scooped them out of the bucket with a strainer and put them back in the tank.

'Makes a little outing for them. Broadens their horizons.' He had quite a gentle speaking voice but his laugh was as loud as a shout. He was endlessly amused by what he saw, heard and thought and it was a noisy business to be in his company.

While he was out of the room emptying the bucket I looked closely at the fish trying to identify the ones who had had their horizons so suddenly broadened. Some of them looked a bit bashed but they were all swimming about quite happily. This was somehow reassuring.

He had, he said, a few questions. If I'd looked forward to telling my life story to an admiring listener, I'd clearly come to the wrong shop.

'When do you start drinking?'

'When I wake up.'

'D'you get through the day without falling over?'

'Yes, I have a job which I do quite well.'

'You mean you think you do it quite well.'

'Well, I haven't got the sack yet.'

'Not yet. What do you do after your waking-up drink?'

'Look for my clothes.'

'D'you remember where you've been the night before?'

'Sometimes.'

'Eat anything?'

'Not much.'

'Let's have a look at your shoes.'

Dr Dent's bedside manner – 'Go back to work on Monday.'

He inspected the tips of the soles and was delighted to find them badly worn away. 'Foot-drop,' he said. 'Bet there's no reaction.' I took off my socks and he brushed the soles of my feet with an upward movement of his hand. 'No reaction!' he crowed. My bona fides seemed to be established by my unresponsive feet.

'Before I commit myself to treating you, I need to know why you want to stop drinking.'

'Well, I suppose it's because I can't. I mean I've tried to drink less, not to drink spirits and . . .'

'Yes, yes, but what I want to know is have you come to me to please someone else? Your long-suffering wife, your poor old mother, your rich boss, dear God, anyone?'

'No, I don't think so. I only decided this morning when I rang you up.'

'Fine. I can't treat people who think they are doing someone else a favour. You need to do it for your own sake. A genuinely selfish act. Today's Wednesday, I could take you in on Friday.'

'Could we make it next Tuesday?'

'Please yourself. A week can be a long time. Come to 99 Cromwell Road at four o'clock.'

'What about the treatment? What is it?'

'Purely chemical. It's not an aversion treatment. Large injections of apomorphine. No psychiatry. I'm not interested in your mind, just in curing your body. Read this book. It'll tell you all you need to know and I can fill you in as we go along. It takes five days – maybe seven if you have a go of DTs. You might or you might not. No bad thing if you do.'

'Convalescence?'

'No! Of course not. You'll feel extremely well. Never better.'

'Oh, and what will it cost?'

'I don't know. You'll have to pay No. 99's charges – fifty quid? The two nurses a fiver a day each. My fee whatever that may be. You'll have to think what you can afford.'

'And there's nothing you want to know about me?'

'No, *thank* you.'

He shouted his laugh all the way to the front door.

'See you next week.' Slam.

As I stood, dazed and delighted, deciding where to go for a celebratory drink, the door opened again and bright blue eyes over half-glasses peered through the white hedge of hair. 'In case you're wondering, I've never killed anyone yet. And if you find you can't last through to Tuesday ring me up. I'll get them to keep a room for Friday just in case.' Slam.

Dr Dent was, of course, quite right and I only just made it to Friday. Once the decision was taken, all my brakes failed and I thankfully abandoned the elaborate little systems of checks and balances by which I usually remained just sober enough to manage a working day. But before the inevitable tidal wave of alcohol enfolded me I had the sense to tell my 'rich boss' and my 'poor old mother' that I was going into hospital for some tests and would be away for a week or ten days. I remember very little about the next 36 hours but some kind friend must have told Dent that I would like to come in on Friday and punctually at four o'clock, pleasantly blotto, I arrived by taxi at 99 Cromwell Road. If the guppies could survive that sort of treatment then so, I thought, could I.

Number 99 Cromwell Road was one of the tall, gloomy, shabby houses which flanked the streams of traffic thronging into and out of London from and to the West of England via Heathrow. It's been pulled down now, like most of its fellows, and replaced by a vast shiny hotel which somehow contrives to retain the air of shabby gloom which is its rightful inheritance. In 1957 it was a private Nursing Home used mostly for abortions, just inside the law, by free-thinking doctors like Ellis Stungo who used to get a lot of outraged publicity but also a lot of customers.

The door was opened by an Irish dragon who offered no welcome. I told her my name and that I was a patient of Dr. Dent's. 'Just stay right where you are and don't go away,' she said, and shut the door in my face. I could hear her calling up the stairs, 'Gibson! Another of your drunks is here. Come and get it.' Sister Gibson arrived quickly, friendly and apologetic. 'Sorry about that. Come on up and have a drink.'

There were five floors and Dent had the call on two rooms on the top floor. The third, much smaller room was occupied permanently by a charming elderly lady, Miss Todhunter, who was fortunately stone deaf. She was quite oblivious to the comings and goings of Dent's patients and the occasional uproars and was on excellent terms with him and with his four regular nurses. She wasn't ill and needed no nursing, but she read a lot, preferred life in bed to trudging about outside and if the food was vile at least she didn't have to cook it.

My room was clean and had a large window looking out on to the Cromwell Road. The bedstead was of solid-looking brass with knobs on the four corners and the mattress was thick and well-sprung to the touch. The bed was turned down and looked quite inviting. Sister Gibson offered gin or whisky and when I chose gin said that I'd better stick to it over the next couple of days. She was writing on the cover of a new blue exercise book.

'I've put you down as Tiger Tim. All very discreet. Most people call me Gibby or Kate.'

I chose Kate and raised no objection to Tiger Tim. I remembered him as a leading character among the animals at Mrs Hippo's school in the main front-page strip cartoon in *Playbox*, the weekly comic to which I'd been addicted as a small child. It seemed a good sign. But what about the gin? I thought this wasn't an aversion treatment.

'No more it is,' she said, 'but we don't want you having withdrawal symptoms until we've got you full of apomorphine, so you'll be needing it. It's all in Dr Dent's book but, of course, you won't have read it. I keep telling him that none of you is going to read it before you come in but he keeps hoping. He'll be in this evening and will tell you how it works.

The main thing is that it does work. The first two days are rough. Injections of apomorphine every two hours followed by some gin which will make you sick. Nothing else to drink and no food, of course. You'll sleep a lot. On the third and fourth day we cut out the alcohol, reduce the strength of the apomorphine injections to a level where you don't even feel sick and increase the intervals to three hours. That's when you may get delusions, mild or otherwise, or indeed you may not. Everyone's different and it doesn't really matter. The fifth day you take apomorphine by mouth just to round it off and you can take me out to Bailey's Hotel for a drink and start practising drinking lemonade yourself. And the next day you go home. That's it, so let's get started.'

When Dent arrived that evening, he was quieter but full of talk and amiable too. He was clearly as much at home here as with his tropical fish. He said that he'd discovered his apomorphine treatment more or less by chance. In the late twenties he'd used it or emetine as an aversion treatment and noticed that he got much better results with apomorphine. One patient did particularly well and he later discovered that he had neither sense of taste nor smell. He realised then that whatever treatment he'd given this man it certainly wasn't any sort of aversion which depended entirely on the patient recoiling instinctively from the smell and taste of alcohol.

Addiction to alcohol, he said, was based on two main things. First, the need for an anaesthetic to obliterate anxiety. If the back (unconscious) brain is in a state of inertia then the pressure on the front (conscious) brain becomes eventually intolerable. Secondly, the gradual change in the chemistry of the body caused by heavy drinking over a long period means, in the end, that it can only extract sugar from alcohol and not from food.

He worked on it over the years and came to the conclusion that apomorphine had the answers to these two problems, quite apart from its superficial role as a powerful emetic. First, it stimulates the body's main nerve centre, the hypothalamus, and in so doing gives the back brain a considerable jolt out of its inertia. Secondly, its effect on the digestive system is to restore the body's natural function of getting sugar from food. With the two parts of the brain once more in balance and the ability to get sugar from food restored, the patient is no longer addicted to alcohol.

He agreed that it all sounded too simple and that he was regarded with hostility by other British doctors in the addiction business, but the fact remained that the treatment worked and when I left No. 99 Cromwell Road I simply wouldn't need alcohol any more. I must never drink it again, but that was common sense and not dependent on any great exercise of will-power. It would take a little time to adjust my habits and find something else to do in the evening, etc. If I drank alcohol by mistake, a tablet of apomorphine under the tongue and an hour or two's sleep would put me right.

It sounded both sensible and dotty at the same time. I can't say that I understood the theory then or now but the same goes for television and radio and I can manage to use both without any trouble. Anyway, I'd already started the treatment and I felt an unreasoning and perhaps unreasonable confidence that all would be well. I feared no evil.

The next two days were really a sort of endurance test – exhausting, uncomfortable and boring. Thirst was the over-riding snag and my aim in life was to reach Sunday afternoon and drink buckets of cold clear water. Sometimes I thought of burying my face in an enormous watermelon. In fact, according to the Tiger Tim record, I slept for 22 out of the 48 hours, so I was blissfully unconscious for nearly half the time. Kate was around all day and the nights were shared by a retired hospital matron, Hannah Mason-Jones, who had nursed for my late and rather grand gynaecologist uncle in Cardiff years ago, and a nice young New Zealander, Dinah, who had never seen an alcoholic at close quarters before. Hannah and I had long chats about my uncle Ewen whom she had firmly planted on a pedestal. Both he and my father, his elder brother, had been life-long teetotallers and she felt that it was up to her to get me into that exclusive club and so save a bit of the family honour. I said that I didn't think that Dent would approve of my going through all this for the sake of the family honour but perhaps it would be OK for me to regard it as a bit of a bonus on the side.

Dent came in two or three times a day, sometimes late at night, and quite soon I began to feel that I'd never really known any other people but these my familiars.

I had my last gin at three o'clock on Sunday afternoon and at four o'clock half a pint of iced water. The best.

Apart from injections every three hours, there was nothing particular I had to do for the next two days and I was curious but not apprehensive about what form the 'mild or otherwise' delusions might take. I could expect anyway to become shaky and perhaps irritable in the process of weathering the withdrawal of the gin. I slept a good deal on Sunday evening and that night I noticed the first oddity. I picked up a green Penguin, one of Simenon's Maigret novels, and the green background turned to brilliant turquoise, the white bits to a violent yellow and the black lettering a phosphorescent royal blue. By next morning the colours were back to normal.

But I was by no means back to normal. The euphoria induced by surviving the first and supposedly worst two days had passed and I felt ill, anxious and very shaky. A few friends dropped in during the afternoon but were not encouraged to linger. Among them were two clergymen and when Kate opened the door to them she exclaimed, 'Christ! He's not that bad.' As soon as the lights were turned on the colours began to change again. We had a most unwelcome visit from the Matron of the Nursing Home who treated us to a lengthy account of her summer holiday in Cornwall. She was a dark, voluble lady wearing a white bonnet tied with a large white bow on the right side of her face and she was leaning on the top rail of the end of my brass bedstead as she brought her grisly narrative to its climax. This concerned the afternoon when a shark had attacked a group of bathers from a beach near her hotel. It managed to mangle a fair portion of a man's leg, she said with a little laugh, 'well up the thigh'. As she gazed at me her bonnet and bow turned bright yellow and her hair royal blue. 'I said to myself, "Whatever next!"' she said. This was exactly what I was thinking, too, because I was hearing faint but insistent voices just above my head and there was background music coming from the area of the window.

Dent came in a little later. He was reassuring but he looked amazing with all that yellow hair and as soon as I lay on my back a vast moving panoramic water scene appeared on the ceiling. I realised that I was losing control of my visual and audio senses and that these were the first of the 'mild or otherwise'. But at least I knew them for what they were.

That night Dinah and I seemed to be in a hotel bedroom and I felt badly about having the only bed. Such chivalrous thoughts fled when the whole room was shaken by a great orange helicopter hovering just outside the window. I sprang out of bed and made for the door but Dinah got there first and I still had enough of a hold on my mind to work through her explanation. The deafening noise was that of two motorbikes revving their engines in the Cromwell Road below and the large wooden cross bars of the window frame, set against the pink and yellow glow from the street lights and the more distant West End, made up my orange helicopter. It seemed a good idea not to look at the window for a bit. However, as I turned my back on it, I was not encouraged to see three small furry animals in the far corner of the room.

By Tuesday morning my fading grasp on reality had gone altogether and I remained trapped in delirium for the next two days and nights.

When I left No. 99 at the end of the week, I decided to write down what I remembered of my adventures and by cross-checking with the laconic entries in the Tiger Tim exercise book which Kate gave to me, I could even get the five main nightmares into some sort of chronological order. Now, 40 years later, they still come vividly to mind, not in the same way as memories of actual happenings, but as if I had read about them happening to someone else. I'm not frightened or shamed by them.

The delusions themselves were, with a few exceptions, commonplace enough – wild animals, snakes, threatening voices, mobs howling for one's blood, carnivorous insects, shame at one's own cowardice, trying always to flee from danger. They contained many of the elements of adventure stories in the *Boys Own Paper* but put together so that the narrator was the complete anti-hero, failing each test and funking each challenge. I knew that my enemies would win every time. If Walter Mitty had had DTs instead of daydreams I daresay that he would have fared no better than I.

But a few of my delusions were neither terrifying nor unpleasant. I recall a most agreeable game of clock golf with my sister on the roof of some high building; and running the 100 yards in my pyjamas and with bare feet in 9.5 seconds (a new world record then) was a splendid achievement.

More interesting, I think, is how Dr Dent and the nurses tried, often successfully, to find out what was happening in my world, and by their words and actions to make things better for me. Whichever of them was present in the room was always a part of my world, although they were never actual doctor or nurse but had parts to play in each dramatic episode. So what they said and did and their support, or the lack of it, was extremely important for good or ill to the course of events. They hardly ever tried to persuade me that what I could see, hear and feel was not real, but simply that with their help I could survive and cope with it. Early on when I was having a problem with rats Dinah, exhausted and exasperated, said 'Look! There *are* no rats.' This temporarily destroyed my confidence in her as an ally. She realised her mistake and teamed up with me again. On the other hand when I had a lot of snakes writhing and biting in the bed, Kate flung back the bed-clothes, grabbed a spare blanket from the cupboard and picked them up one by one and, after checking with me that there was none left, bundled them up in the blanket, opened the door and threw it out into the passage. A great success.

But, of course, events often moved very quickly in my world and it was difficult for them to keep abreast of new and dangerous developments. Dent and I were having tea in a recently bombed zoo in which many of the cages had been destroyed. We were in the remains of an enclosure and were delighted to find some Aberdeen terrier puppies and gave them some of our jam sandwiches. At this point two hungry pumas arrived on the scene, ate the puppies and turned towards us. Dent, of course, was unaware of this development and went on placidly offering jam sandwiches. When I shouted that he was now feeding pumas instead of scotties, he said firmly that all pumas loved jam sandwiches and proved it by leading the pumas, as they munched their sandwiches, out of the room. My relief was short-lived because he had entirely failed to notice a wounded lioness dragging herself across the floor towards us. As I made for the door Dent and I collided and a brief wrestling match took place. I had no time to tell him about the lioness and simply yelled that we had to get out. As we fought (naturally he didn't want me loose in the passage) I told him he was an old man and could die if he liked but I was off. I don't know how he pacified me but to do so he must have discovered the lioness in my life and shooed her off the scene. Perhaps he fed her jam sandwiches too.

At least two of the main narratives were set in or around the derelict zoo, but the first drama was certainly the siege of our room in 99 Cromwell Road. There was a noisy hostile mob outside and the building had already been infiltrated by violent, implacable dwarves who were responsible for letting quantities of rats, snakes, red ants, scorpions and the like into the room to flush us out into the street below. An entry in Tiger Tim's log reads:

'Patient seeing animals, rats, monkeys and dwarves sitting on the sofa . . . Patient rather frightened.'

My terror, at this stage, had not entirely paralysed me and I snatched up Kate's red silk umbrella to defend us against the rats. Before she could stop me I was out of the door and along the passage pursuing the rats into Miss Todhunter's room and out again. They told her later that I'd come to read the electricity meter and had mistaken the room. I hope she believed them. I did at least one rat to death in one of my own shoes in the cupboard and very nasty it was. I also broke Kate's umbrella in the process.

During the siege I could hear a loud-speaker out in the Cromwell Road describing accurately my reactions to the various horrors going on. I couldn't think how they knew until I observed the activities of a group of mice on the dressing table near the window. They had ingeniously pushed the swing mirror at an angle to catch the sun and were heliographing the news to their comrades out in the road. Kate scooped them up in her useful blanket and chucked them out of the window and the broadcast shut off at once.

Apart from my domestic and local difficulties, there were long sequences abroad and we must have travelled thousands of miles trying to avoid my personal 'Appointment in Samara'. We were pursued across Europe by a band of European Free Knights who bombarded us with steel arrows from a sort of pom-pom gun; stalked by a giant bald French-speaking Negro, armed with a great wooden stave, through dark Brussels streets; and interrogated endlessly by the KGB and their Chinese counterparts in Moscow and Peking.

'Blood, swords and fighting everywhere . . .' according to the Tiger Tim record. But we eventually got to New Zealand where things were much less hectic and Dinah even visited her parents and I saw my brother Andy and his wife and children.

Towards the end of the delirium there was a long, peaceful episode in which Dent and I and Hannah, dressed as a nun, boarded quite a comfortable boat whose destination was death. It stopped from time to time and people got on and off. At each stop my brother Donald appeared, sometimes accompanied by his sons, and urged me to get off and catch a later boat. He said they went all the time. Bertrand Russell was there, scribbling away at his desk in a corner of the bar. He claimed that he was 'past all this death business' and travelled the route back and forth to get his writing done. Anyway Dent and Hannah, the nun, and I decided to stay on board as death seemed to be quite an acceptable and even agreeable end to all our adventures. We held hands, said what prayers we could remember and, as the oxygen ran out, the last thing I remember was the grip of their hands loosening.

I found only one reference towards the end of the Tiger Tim record to '*lots of praying . . .*', so I later asked Dent whether I'd looked like dying at some point in these two days. He said no. He'd thought that they might have to interrupt the delirium if it went on too long, partly because of the strain on me and partly because they were getting seriously exhausted. It would have been quite easy to achieve by giving me several large gins but it would have meant starting all over again at a later date and anyway it was good for me to get all the horrors out. They were pumping apomorphine into me as often as they dared and sooner or later I'd come out of it. And so I did.

I woke up early on Thursday morning and there was Kate.

'So you're back, are you? About time but you're welcome all the same.'

I cautiously raised an arm, extended my fingers and held it there. Not a tremor. 'It's nice to be back,' I said. 'Where's Henry?' (At some point and for some reason Dent had become Henry to me and Henry he remained until he died five years later.) 'Sleeping it off I hope. The poor brute's only had three hours' sleep in the last two days thanks to you and your antics. But never mind, he'll be in later.'

Thursday was a day of rest for us all. I sucked a few apomorphine tablets and on Friday I took Kate out to the bar at Bailey's Hotel, filled her up and drank the first of I don't know how many tonic waters. It must run into tens of thousands by now. Before I left on Saturday, my thirty-third birthday, Henry gave me half-an-hour's 'waking suggestion'. He explained that it was a mild form of hypnosis. He gave me a copy of *The Times* and told me to read the leaders aloud while he was talking to me. He would be telling me things of an encouraging nature which I wanted to hear, e.g. I would have no need at all for alcohol, etc. If he suggested something which I didn't like I would stop reading at once. I don't know what he said to me so I can't judge its effect but I didn't stop reading aloud at all. Henry was very keen on it and said that provided there was mutual trust between giver and receiver it was a useful bit of back-up.

I also asked Henry if he was sure that I shouldn't have just a few days' convalescence. 'No, no, no!' he shouted. 'You've had your convalescence – a nice free trip around the world. You've got a job. Go back to work on Monday.'

So I went back to work on Monday morning ready to start my strange new sober life. I rather spoiled my entrance by slipping on the grand front staircase, but I think it was just a reminder of things past.

Postscript

Maurice Macmillan kept a beady, bloodshot eye on me for the next few weeks and gave regular bulletins to his wife Katie. He'd written an encouraging letter to me at the Cromwell Road and when I came out I gave him a full but slightly bowdlerised account of my adventures. I never suggested that he might like to give it a go himself. Too many people had been telling him what he ought to do for far too long. But every few days he asked me if it was much of a struggle not to drink, and I always replied truthfully that it didn't seem to be a struggle at all. So I wasn't really surprised when, a week before Christmas, he telephoned to say that he'd just arrived at 99 Cromwell Road and that he was starting the treatment in about half an hour.

Katie told me that the day before he'd said that I had the weakest character of all his friends and if Dent's treatment worked for me there was no reason why it shouldn't work for him too. He'd telephoned to Henry, seen him later that morning and there he was – no consultation with her, his GP, his family or friends or with me. He just decided to do it.

I looked in to see him that evening. He was in the other room on the fifth floor and looked after by Henry's other pair of veteran nurses. One of them said, 'We've told him that Miss Todhunter's out of bounds.' 'Tough luck,' I said, 'best part.'

Maurice completed the course in five days flat with no DTs at all, though he claimed a couple of minor fits. He went home on Christmas Eve and died sober 25 years later.

12. *Life After Dent*

I felt quite timid in the first days back. I wasn't worrying so much about reaching for the bottle – indeed the cupboard where I kept the drink was as I'd left it the previous week. When I said to Henry that I supposed it would be sensible to get rid of it he was most indignant. 'Certainly not. Keep it by you. Don't be frightened of it; you'll find that you can live perfectly happily with alcohol all round you without the slightest danger that you'll feel the need to drink it. If you've *got* any sensible friends, go to pubs, clubs, whatever with them and make sure they drink what they want and you'll find they'll relax and thankfully treat you like a human being. You'll find all sorts of new things to enjoy and that's one of them. If you like you can come with me to the next Savage Club Guest Night.'

What was making me timid was the realisation that I now had great acres of time to fill, particularly in the evenings and at night if I didn't sleep. Sleeping pills were taboo. 'Not even an aspirin,' said Henry. 'If you can't get to sleep at first, read a book or write a book or go for a walk or do some work. Just remember that sleeping is something you have to do in the end – like breathing. Your body just needs a little time to adjust. It'll come right.'

Quite soon I found a temporary solution to the problem of evenings on my own. I was living in Oakley Street in Chelsea, quite near the old Pier Hotel where you could eat in the saloon bar (commonplace now but hard to find reasonably cheap and edible pub food in the evening then). There were always quite a lot of people but it was only really crowded at the weekend. So I used to go there when I came home from work, have something to eat and settle down in a corner with a large tonic water which I topped up from time to time and read a book until closing time at 11 p.m. The Pier had not been a haunt of mine and when occasionally I caught the eye of acquaintances at the bar I found that a cheerful wave was enough to satisfy convention and I could return to my book and tonic. I gained great comfort by just being there, surrounded by familiar noise, smoke and smells. I was a passive item in the scene, like an extra in a film.

Of course I didn't do this every evening and I went to a lot of movies with friends. The first one was on the afternoon I left the Cromwell Road and the friend who had very decently come to collect me suggested we went to something funny and took me off to the film of one of Richard Gordon's books *Doctor at Sea*. The opening sequence happens to be of the ship's carpenter in the throes of DTs and running amok with an axe. I didn't mind that but I suddenly realised that my companion was rigid with horror. I told him that it wasn't a patch on the real thing.

My date with Henry came up all too soon. I was never any good at parties, drunk or sober, but Henry couldn't have known that so it was going to be even more of a test than he'd intended. Savage Guest Nights were (and I'm sure still are) sociable affairs. Drink flowed before, during and after dinner and the entertainment was provided by the members themselves, many of whom were professional actors and musicians. That night the fare ranged from stand-up comics to Yehudi Menuhin playing his fiddle. It was a friendly, noisy occasion and Henry loved it. His laughter was just part of the general hubbub. He wasn't a teetotaller but he drank very little alcohol of any sort. I think he had one glass of wine but he'd ordered several bottles of Swiss apple juice and he and I drank a lot of that. I thought longingly of my corner in the Pier, but it was important to me to get through the evening without flinching and to have appeared not to enjoy it would have been very rude into the bargain. A few months later I put myself through the much worse ordeal of a Regimental Dinner just to check that I could.

I was sitting next to Eustace Pett, a retired conductor of choirs and an old friend of Henry's. He was a cheerful old gent with flowing white hair, goatee and moustaches. He enjoyed himself so much that his pleasure was almost infectious and I was really grateful to him for it. When the proceedings came to an end Henry announced casually that we would run Eustace home and then he'd drop me off in Oakley Street.

I'd never driven with Henry but I felt in my bones that he'd be a terrible driver so I clambered quickly into the back of his battered Morris Minor and prayed that the journey would be quick. But of course the Savage was then in Carlton House Terrace SW1 and the Petts lived at least seven miles away in SE23. Henry drove every bit as badly as I feared but he clearly enjoyed it. Red lights were only recognised at the last minute and each shuddering halt was accompanied by shouts of 'Whoa'. I can't believe that he deliberately aimed the car at every bump and hole in the road but he certainly can't have missed many and as our heads banged up against the roof he shouted things like 'Hold on!' and 'Mind out!' I once asked how many accidents he'd had to which he replied 'None.' I let it go, but perhaps he just never noticed them. We had tea with the Petts and it was after midnight when he got me to my front door with a final stamp on the brakes. As I said goodbye and thank you he said, 'Come to No. 99 tomorrow (Sunday) at about four. Someone for you to meet.'

That night for the first time since my return I fell at once into a deep peaceful sleep. Earned the hard way.

Next day I rang the doorbell of No. 99 and the Irish dragon let me in with a vicious cackle. 'That didn't last long. Gibson!' And there was Kate leaning over the bannisters just as she had been a fortnight and a world ago. 'Come on up.'

It was strange to walk into 'my' room and to see a total stranger in 'my' bed. He was sitting bolt upright, ashen-faced, long-nosed, mouth and eyes little more than pencilled in and his thin greyish hair cropped. Henry was there fiddling with some notes at the same table from which he'd dispensed jam sandwiches to the pumas. 'Hope you slept well,' he said and the laugh ricocheted round the high, familiar walls. The figure in the bed remained motionless and Kate introduced us. 'This darling is Alan Maclean and this darling is William Burroughs and he's written a book called *The Naked Lunch* and I'm sure you're going to publish it for him.' Burroughs came slowly to life and asked who I worked for. When I said, 'Macmillan' he managed a smile of genuine amusement.

'I'd love to read it.'

'I really don't think you would.' The smile was still there.

'Try me.'

'Well, I'll send you a copy from Paris if I ever get out of here. Though I doubt it will pass your Customs.'

I had a colleague whose standard response to typescripts which he felt were a bit 'off colour' was a lofty 'Hardly Ours'. I visualised an editorial meeting with the typescript of *The Naked Lunch* on the table steaming gently like a pile of fresh manure beneath the offended nostrils of my colleagues. 'Hardly Ours' would barely cover the reaction, I thought.

Henry said he'd have Burroughs right in about a week. He was going to treat his heroin addiction in exactly the same way as he'd treated mine to alcohol and the result would be just as good. We must have looked doubtful because he added, 'Look, you don't have to like each other; alcoholics and drug addicts nearly always despise each others' addictions. Remember the Pharisee who fell to his knees praising God that he was not like other men? Well as far as I, apomorphine and probably God, if you think He exists, are concerned, you and your addictions are much of a muchness. And I wanted Burroughs to see someone who's recently had the treatment so that he could judge the result for himself.'

Burroughs and I looked at each other sheepishly. I wondered if he was scheduled for a night out with the Savages but just said that I felt fine and strongly recommended the good doctor and all his works. I don't know how impressed Burroughs was by my appearance and performance but he was entertained by the Macmillan connection and it looked as though he and Henry were going to get along. So we said polite goodbyes.

Henry was as good as his word and Burroughs returned to Paris in a week, leaving his addiction behind him. But I never got my copy of *The Naked Lunch*. In the copy I bought in London the other day there is an appreciative note in the introduction about Henry and his treatment.

I don't think that either of them would have had the faintest idea of how to conform to the *mores* of the conventional mainstreams of their separate worlds even if they'd wanted to. It's true that Burroughs's books are in print in many different languages and that he has 'guru' status in his native America, so presumably he is in grave danger of inadvertently setting standards for others – an evolution not much to his liking, I suspect.

I went to see Burroughs about 20 years ago when he had a flat off Jermyn Street in London. There didn't seem to be much in the way of furniture except a couple of chairs and what looked like an aluminium igloo. We sat on the chairs with our backs to the igloo and chatted about Henry for an hour or so. I wanted him to write a book about Dent and in particular about their collaboration. He was friendly and said that he'd already published some admiring references to Dent and apomorphine but he didn't know much about Dent's life or career and he hadn't really much else to say. I told him about the vast sprawling mass of unfinished memoirs chiefly about his early years as a medical student and as a young GP. It was often fascinating and funny but unpublishable on its own.

Maurice and I had tried to persuade Dent to bring it up to date but his heart wasn't in it and it didn't amuse him. But it will one day be a rich seam to mine. I wasn't surprised that Burroughs turned me down and he promised that if I ever found a good biographer he'd be glad to talk to him or her.

I acted as 'After' in 'Before and After' for several more of Henry's patients and the Irish dragon and I became almost friendly. The matron with the shark bedtime story had moved on but Miss Todhunter remained a peaceful oasis on the fifth floor. Later Henry and his nurses abandoned No. 99 and moved to a slightly grander nursing home in one of the handsome squares leading off the Kings Road in Chelsea. The supporting cast of characters changed but the Irish dragon's replacement had some of her predecessor's infallible touch for making new patients expect nothing but the worst. She was a cosy old thing and a mine of misinformation lovingly imparted. Her favourite and most successful ploy was to warn incoming patients not to lean too heavily on a section of the banisters between the ground and first floors. 'It's loose, dear.' If, as she hoped, the patient asked why, she said casually, 'It comes apart, dear, so they can get the coffins down.' It seldom failed.

Henry and I became friends and met often. When I moved to a basement flat in South Kensington he and Kate came and installed a modest-sized tropical fish tank and stocked it with a few guppies from his own herd – perhaps the direct descendants of the ones I had first observed having their horizons broadened. Guppies breed very fast and very often and the population is kept down to manageable numbers by a simple process of cannibalism. As the mother guppy ejects her babies they provide an immediate snack for the uncles and aunts who have been swimming close by for this purpose. The few survivors join the game if and when they grow up. I added some exotica later but none of them appeared to breed at all.

In the interests of our friendship I managed to get through several more Savage Club Guest Nights, but by that time I had an old car of my own and was allowed to drive Henry and Eustace home afterwards. He also met my mother and became a regular visitor. She was good company and also the proud possessor of most of the 'proper' wooden jigsaw puzzles from The Bee's lending library and nearly always had one on the go. Among Henry's idiosyncrasies was an affectionate respect for failed solo commercial enterprises and he listened enthralled (he claimed) to the history of The Bee's ups and downs. Anyway, he called himself the only honorary subscriber and went nearly every week to return a puzzle and take out a new one and of course to have a cup of tea and a chat.

I went into hospital and had my gall bladder removed on Christmas Eve 1961. Something went a bit wrong and my recovery took much longer than advertised. After leaving the hospital I went to recuperate in the country. I'd already lent my flat to Frank Tuohy, who faithfully fed and hoovered the tropical fish but he had to move on before I was well enough to return to London. I telephoned Henry to ask if he could take in my fish as lodgers and discovered that he was very ill and of course he couldn't take them. Frank managed to find homes for all the fish before he left. Somehow I'd never connected Henry with his own mortality and his death a short time later was a most unwelcome shock and grief. Sometimes friendships have a discernible pattern and I remember thinking at the time that guppies were the Alpha and Omega of ours. Now almost forty years later I think of him often and whenever I come across a tank of tropical fish I salute it.

Unlike Burroughs, Henry never became a national guru and his apomorphine treatment is not, as far as I know, in use anywhere. Although he had belonged to the Society for the Study of Addiction for many years and had been both Secretary of the Society and the editor of its journal, most of his peers regarded him as an iconoclastic eccentric. Even those who liked and even admired him as a man did not take apomorphine seriously. He was a hero only to his nurses and to his patients to whom he restored their lives as good as new, and most of us are now dead. It still seems mad to me that his treatment has been allowed to die with him and that no one has had even the curiosity to disinter it and give it a trial. The need for quick, effective and cheap treatment for addiction of all kinds has never been greater. The last article he wrote describing the treatment and how he discovered and developed it appeared in *The Medical Press* in May 1961 and is reprinted as an appendix at the back of this book.

But he would be hugely pleased to know that his beloved apomorphine has once again been 'discovered' – this time as a new and startlingly successful element in the treatment of Parkinson's Disease.

So perhaps he'll have the last laugh yet. Earplugs all round in the Elysian Fields.

13. *Mr Harold & Son*

Harold Macmillan's return to publishing in the winter of 1963 after seven years as Prime Minister was the beginning of a difficult and depressing time for him and a difficult and alarming time for us.

Maurice had succeeded Mr Dan as Chairman in the spring of that year and the first thing he did was to make the unassuming but able Frank Whitehead his Chief Executive/General Manager. Together they took a major plunge by starting to build a new warehouse-cum-offices in Basingstoke, to be followed in due course by the sale of the old premises in St Martin's Street and the renting of a London office. But a few days after his father's resignation Maurice was promoted from the Back Benches to be one of the Treasury ministers in Alec Douglas-Home's government and accordingly left the firm as his father re-entered it. So inside one year we had three successive chairmen and had taken the first steps towards a massive physical upheaval. By this time Maurice and I had been sober for six years and Frank, Rex Allen and I had been directors for less than a year.

Mr Harold was still a sick and exhausted man when he left hospital and formally became our new chairman. His doctors advised him that he should give himself plenty of time to recuperate and he confined himself to a single visit to the office, during which he instructed us to carry on with whatever we might be doing and said he expected to be fit enough to take up the reins in the New Year. Sure enough he reappeared early in January recovered in health if not in spirits and ready for action.

Most of those who had worked for him before were confident that he would lead us into the Promised Land. I hardly knew him but had met him once or twice with Maurice and had been touched and flattered by a letter he wrote to me in his own hand in 1955 when he was Foreign Secretary. He wrote it the day before he announced in the House of Commons that the Government now had evidence (provided by a Soviet defector) that Donald and Guy Burgess had been long-term Soviet agents. Up to this point succeeding Labour and Conservative governments had blandly maintained that they didn't know where they had gone or why. This was not exactly a widely held view, so the announcement caused no surprise and simply set the parliamentary record straight. But I thought and think that it was a very kindly act to write the letter. He said among other things that he felt sure that the time would come when I would be able to forget the nightmare, or look back upon it as hardly belonging to me at all – just an event in the past.

But that was nine years earlier and I didn't altogether share the general feeling of euphoria at the prospect of Supermac at the helm. After all, he had been for seven years one of the most important men in the world and I wondered how he would adapt to coming down to our level. What would he think of us and what would he expect of us? The answers to these questions proved to be 'Not much' and 'Quite a lot'. He was deeply unimpressed by what he found. He was also unaware of how much and in what ways the book trade had changed in the post-war years, which made it impossible to wave a magic wand and make things, overnight, more to his liking.

No one could have accused us of being up-to-date in our methods and practices and although we were beginning to catch on and to catch up a bit, there was a yawning gap between us and the leading performers in the trade. I have to admit too that, although I was (and still am) proud of the authors whose books we had published in the last ten years, my chief source of enjoyment had been the wonderful untrammelled eccentricities of Mr Dan. I wasn't at all sure that I would have such a good time under the new regime. Somehow I couldn't see Mr Harold running down the directors' corridor waving a novel and shouting, 'Who is responsible for this disgusting book?'

But Harold was not at first so much concerned with our antiquated systems and our lowish profile in the trade. He just thought we were wet, boring and above all unprofitable. So the six non-family directors were at the sharp end of his displeasure and at one moment it looked as though he might dispense with the services of all but one of us, thus handing back administrative control to the last stalwart of the Old Guard (already close to retirement) with whom he shared memories of the firm in palmier days as well as a low opinion of the rest of us. He held a dismal series of short meetings at which he placed the favoured stalwart in a chair to the right of his desk and had us, the goats, seated in a semi-circle in front of him.

When he had concluded his survey of our activities we were all except the sheep-stalwart groggily on the defensive if not actually in the dock. He promised to talk to each of us individually in due course.

My turn came quite soon. He said obliquely that Rache had had a good innings and paused impressively to let me digest that. He went on to say that Rache had decided to retire a bit ahead of time – 'Books of his own to write and so on.' He didn't specify what sort of batting error had brought this good innings to a close, but I had no doubt that Harold had been both the bowler and the umpire. I waited to hear my fate. 'I think,' he said slowly, 'that you'd better take over.' I said, 'Ah', thinking rightly that there was more to come. 'After all, there comes a time when you either have to get on or get out.' I waited to see if there was anything more to be had in the way of encouragement, but he'd clearly shot his bolt in that department; I thanked him and retreated from the presence.

I found Rache in his office. 'Have you seen Harold?' I nodded. 'Did he give you the job?' 'Yes I think so,' aping the master, 'but he sounded as if he wished he hadn't. But I need to know if this is really what you want?' 'Yes, it is, I promise you and you'll get on fine. I'll write to my authors and you'll find that they'll all be happy to work with you.' 'Even Rebecca West?' 'Yes, even Rebecca.'

My doubts about Rebecca's likely reaction to the news that henceforth she would have to deal with me had their roots in a bizarre incident several years before. Rache had asked her to come and talk to our assembled salesmen about her forthcoming novel *The Fountain Overflows.* These sales meetings took place in the boardroom two or three times a year when Rache, aided by me and Rex, harangued the sales force on the virtues of books scheduled for publication in the next few months.

When the time came for Rebecca to do her stuff I went down to the front hall where she was waiting. I escorted her up the grand staircase and into the boardroom where she was greeted by Rache and took her place at the end of the table beside her. She was very good at this sort of thing and had them eating out of her hand. She made them laugh, they loved the book and their applause when she finished was genuinely enthusiastic. I then escorted her back down the grand staircase, got her a taxi and that was that – or so I thought.

Two years later I met, at some party, a sparky old journalist friend of

Rebecca's, Barbara Back. She asked me who I was and when I told her my name and that I worked for Macmillan she let out a hoot of delight.

'You must be the one who stole Rebecca's typescript!'

'I don't think so,' I said cautiously.

'Well, *she* thinks so!'

I lost her in the crowd before I could find out more.

Next day I tackled Rache and asked him if he knew what I was meant to have done and when. He looked a bit sheepish. 'Oh you mean that ridiculous fuss about the extra chapter for *The New Meaning of Treason*. She thought she'd given it to you to give to me when she came to talk to the travellers.'

'Well, she didn't.'

'I know, I know. And she didn't give it to me either. Must have left it in the taxi.'

She'd rung up Rache the next day to ask him what he thought of it and of course he said he hadn't got it. She came rushing round to the office with another copy and then told him of her dark suspicions that I had destroyed the first one. The new chapter included a few pages about Donald and that was a good enough motive for the theft. Mr Dan had joined the fray and eventually she calmed down and admitted that she couldn't actually remember having given the package to me nor having told me what was in it. So she reluctantly withdrew the charge.

'Why didn't you tell me?'

'Dan and I thought there was no point in upsetting you. And she must have realised that she'd made a complete ass of herself.'

'It looks to me as though she's still dining out on it.'

'I don't think so. I'd have heard about it and she's never raised it with me again.'

I finally read the chapter when the book was published in 1964 by Viking in America. They kindly and innocently sent me a copy of the specially bound edition 'For friends of the author and publishers'.

I looked after Rebecca's books for nearly 20 years and the affair of the missing chapter was never mentioned between us. But I sometimes wondered if she suspected me of other no less bizarre crimes against her. She saw conspiracies in almost every part of her private life as well as in the political and social world outside. For as long as I knew her the domestic conspiracies were mostly connected to her endless feud with Anthony

West, her son by H. G. Wells. But none of her friends and acquaintances was immune from the danger of being cast in a treacherous role in one of her besetting dramas. Many of her letters and telephone calls to me began with the words, 'Something strange and unfortunate has happened . . .' and it's true that a lot of happenings in her life were exactly that, without any underlying conspiracies real or imagined. But conspiracies were what she liked best.

She was a wonderfully good writer and, until old age and illness finally caught up with her, there can hardly have been a day when she wasn't writing. Drafts of books in various stages of construction, reviews, articles, diaries, bits of memoirs and a vast flow of handwritten letters kept her on the boil. She was a literary volcano in almost continuous eruption. She was also a great telephoner, particularly in her last years, and had long daily conversations with a few old friends, thus keeping up her intake and output of political and personal gossip.

She was formidable, unpredictable, entertaining and so clever that I never quite lost the fear of making a fool of myself when talking to her. Ignorance in a conversation with her was never bliss and as she grew deafer she acquired a new disconcerting habit. She would often interrupt one by shouting, 'Wha-at?', but one could never be quite sure that this was just a request to speak up and repeat what one had said. It could just as well have been an expression of amazement and outrage and meant that she thought one was talking nonsense. They both sounded the same. I like to think that she didn't know that she sometimes frightened me. Slowly we became friends and I always looked forward to seeing her.

After her death in 1983 I was looking through some of her notebooks and came across an undated, isolated sentence which read, 'I have come to the conclusion that Alan Maclean is on my side after all and I shall ask him to be one of my literary executors' – which she did. I was glad to know that I had at some unspecified time passed some unspecified test, but the 'after all' bit struck a chill note.

With Rache's sudden departure I found myself in much closer contact with the boss. He wasn't exactly unfriendly but he wanted his pound of flesh from General Books and this meant both staff cuts and a process of weeding out financially unsuccessful authors. Rache had recently taken on a bright young woman to build up the Children's Books list and her job was the first casualty. I wasn't forbidden to publish new children's books so the likes of Rumer Godden and Geoffrey Trease were safe enough and we kept the list going as best we could.

One of the two younger editors had already decided to leave for a better-paid job elsewhere and was not replaced, so we were back to two commissioning editors instead of four, the same number as we'd had when I'd joined Rache ten years before. The policy of weeding out loss-making books and their authors could be loosely implemented by taking on fewer books. But it gave me the opportunity to say that unless we recruited someone to build an up-to-date organisation to market our books abroad as well as at home the odds would be in favour of my getting out rather than on. Harold let that pass and I could almost hear the click as he switched off.

He decided to come to one of our weekly meetings 'just to get the feel of things.' These were still held in the boardroom on Wednesday at 11 o'clock, but Rex, Tim Farmiloe and I were now the only survivors of Mr Dan's motley crew. His impatient ghost was in our minds if not in evidence as we waited in silence for his brother. It felt rather like 11 o'clock at the Cenotaph on Armistice Day. I couldn't take my eyes off the open door in the hope that there might be a mighty rushing wind to announce that Mr Dan was back to reclaim his old stamping ground. No such luck and under Harold's cold magisterial eye we ploughed our way through what we still called Mr Mark's pile. After an hour or so he wished us luck and left us to get on with it. He never came again.

It seemed like months but it can only have been a matter of weeks before a gradual thaw in the atmosphere became apparent. Perhaps by a process of osmosis combined with his own inquisitions Harold had acquired a serviceable knowledge of the state of his firm and had decided which nettles, great or small, he would grasp and in which order. But the really good news was that he had taken Frank Whitehead (Maurice's own choice as Chief Executive) out of the goats' enclosure and clasped him to his bosom, leaving the sheep-stalwart to coast to an honourable retirement.

Frank had been terrified of Mr Dan, distrustful of Rache and often maddened by Maurice's absences on political business when critical decisions about the building of the Basingstoke complex had to be taken. However, he'd kept his nerve and on occasion taken the decisions himself. I'd come to admire his courage and common sense and he clearly had administrative skills of a high order. He was a modest, likeable man driven not by great personal ambition but by a strong preference for seeing things done right. He never thought of himself as a publisher but believed that his job was to create the conditions in which publishing could thrive. Maurice had understood him and valued him but I'd suspected that the handover from son to father had been at best perfunctory, possibly non-existent, and the danger that Harold would misread and discard him had been real enough. I could hardly believe that things could change so suddenly and it was not until I heard Harold address him as 'Dear boy' that I knew we could breathe again. They got on famously.

Harold was obviously feeling much better and beginning to enjoy himself and the mood spread through St Martin's Street. We all walked a bit taller, boasted to our friends in the book trade and at home about the hazards and pleasures of working with Supermac. Almost all our authors liked the idea of being published by him and it was a distinct plus with literary agents and booksellers. The only major exception was John Le Carré who had decided to change publishers after falling out with Victor Gollancz, who had published his first best-seller, *The Spy Who Came in from the Cold*. Every publisher in London wanted him, but I knew that we'd made it to the short list, so we were in with a chance. However, the agent rang me up at the end of a week to say that we were out. He was sorry but the thought of being published by Harold Macmillan had stuck in his author's gullet. I was disappointed but not displeased in a contrary sort of way. I didn't tell anyone in the office the reason given. I thought I'd keep it to myself against a rainy day.

My own relationship with Harold had been improved by the thaw but his new buoyant mood did not extend to any great confidence in me. However, I had the typescript of C. P. Snow's new novel, *Corridors of Power*. There was a lot of parliamentary stuff in it and Charles Snow had already asked Harold to read it and check it for political howlers. Charles and his novelist wife Pamela Hansford-Johnson had been friends and supporters of mine for some years and were generous and optimistic about my elevation. When Charles and Harold went through the typescript together I think that Charles must have put in a good word for me because Harold came and sat in my office to have a chat about the book and its prospects. It wasn't by any means Charles's best novel but, with a General Election looming and his stock still high with literary editors, reviewers and book-sellers, a best-seller was a possibility.

'How many do you think you'll sell?' he enquired. I said I'd be disappointed if it were fewer than 20,000 but . . .

'But what?'

'But if Collins, or Heinemann, or Hodder (who all know how to sell books) had it they'd expect to do a lot more.'

He thought for a bit and then said that if I felt like that I'd better do something about it. 'Talk to Frank.'

I had of course talked to Frank many times but we'd agreed there was no point in pursuing it while our own futures were at best uncertain. Eventually we were going to need someone to become Sales Director for the whole firm, but our immediate need was for new blood in the marketing of General Books and this more modest plan had now miraculously been blessed.

After one or two false starts the name of Nicholas Byam Shaw came up. He was, according to my information, destined for stardom in the Collins Sales firmament but had been temporarily side-tracked by Billy Collins himself who didn't like his protégés to be too successful too soon.

Nicky and I met in the house of a mutual friend in Godalming on a cold wet evening and when he left three hours later I had no doubt that he was the man for us. Frank and I had several more meetings with him and he decided to throw in his lot with ours. Billy was outraged when he resigned and set to work to make him change his mind. He could be formidably and tenaciously persuasive and I held my breath off and on for a few days. But it was too late and Nicky held firm. Billy then turned his fire on to me, rang me up on Maundy Thursday and let loose a torrent of reproachful abuse. He would of course be complaining to Harold Macmillan. Did he knew about it? 'Yes, of course he does,' I lied and hung up. I bolted down the corridor to warn Harold to expect an infuriated Billy on the line. When I'd finished my hurried explanation he looked approvingly at me for the first time since his return. 'Oh, good. If he rings me up I shall come the old Prime Minister on him.' But Billy never rang.

Not long after this Harold decided to take up Maurice's seat on the Pan board. At that time Pan was owned jointly by Macmillan and Collins who each appointed three directors in addition to the Pan working directors. I'd been one of the Macmillan directors since 1962 and Frank had recently taken over from Rache. Having Supermac as a colleague not only transformed our team but also brought out the Stage-door Johnny in everyone else. I basked in his reflected limelight for the two years in which he chose to remain on the board and I used to say such things as 'I'm not too sure that Harold will like that, but I'll have a word with him if you're keen . . .'.

More interestingly Billy never made any effort to dislodge Harold from the No. 1 spot. It had never occurred to me that Billy could be subdued by anyone or anything, but it seemed that he was genuinely a little in awe of the old maestro. Much to Harold's regret he never mentioned the poaching of Byam Shaw and he even gave up telling his favourite old story of how Macmillan had cheated him out of the contract for *Gone With the Wind* in 1936. In fact they got on perfectly well and Billy appeared to be as interested in and amused by his new colleague as anyone else. He also went out of his way to be civil to me so he must have re-arranged things in his mind to his own satisfaction.

Byam Shaw was a success from the start and we sold over 50,000 copies of *Corridors of Power* when we published it a few days after the General Election that autumn. Nicky became Sales Director for the whole company within a year of his arrival and went on, at a more leisurely pace, to the top where he still presides. Harold came to think he was a genius.

One evening in Harold's office when we were quietly congratulating ourselves on the success of Snow's novel, he paused to say, 'Don't call me Sir, dear boy.' I took this to mean that I could now get on with getting on and forget about getting out.

Once he'd satisfied himself that things were moving in the right direction Harold got down to work on his memoirs. He intended to follow Churchill's example and write a combination of autobiography and history. Lord Thompson, who then owned both *The Times* and *The Sunday Times*, bought the British and Commonwealth rights for a large undisclosed sum which reflected Harold's proviso that his own firm should be allowed to contract for the book rights for a comparatively modest advance. The original plan was for three volumes but it soon became clear that he was going to need at least five and the final tally was six. He set up shop at Birch Grove where he had all his papers and came up to the office once or twice a week. He began to write *The Winds of Change* in the late summer of 1964 and the last volume, *At the End of the Day,* was published nine years and well over a million words later. It was an astonishing achievement and he was much indebted to his research assistant, Anne Glyn-Jones, whose administration was as impeccable as her research. His method of work was to dictate a version of each chapter and then to revise the typescript by hand, which in turn became the first and often the final draft. The typescript which reached us was immaculate and his corrections to the book proofs minimal. Commercially all the books did well and two of them, the first and the last, were genuine best-sellers.

Inevitably when you are publishing a sequence of long books at intervals of about 18 months, there is the danger that public interest – and consequently sales – will flag and sag. That this did not happen to any serious extent was due to the hour-long television interviews which were timed to coincide with book publication.

The first of these was the least good but Harold was already an accomplished performer on the box and the programme was widely watched, admired and enjoyed. The BBC was feeling its way and had chosen to have no less than three interlocutors which made it more of a question and answer panel with Harold in the hot seat. When they switched to tête-a-têtes with Robert McKenzie, Professor of Sociology and Politics at the London School of Economics as well as a well-known broadcaster, the effect was electric. The relaxed, informal atmosphere of the drawing room at Birch Grove suited Harold's gifts as a raconteur (as opposed to his gifts as an orator) and his spontaneous wit informed anecdote and exposé alike. Bob McKenzie's self-effacing skill in steering him through each book was brilliant and they made a great team. When the books were finished they resumed their partnership on several occasions in later years.

Harold became through these programmes a television star and they brought him a new affection as well as the admiration of millions of viewers. I went with him to Lime Grove to see a preview of one of them and afterwards, as we were having a drink with McKenzie and Margaret Douglas, the producer, the famous comedians Morecambe and Wise came over from a nearby table to congratulate him on his professionalism and on his timing. One of them added, with a straight face, that television had made them and if he was lucky it might well be the making of him too. On the way back to the office he affected not to know who they were.

Harold's well-known appetite for reading was undiminished (until his last years when his eyesight failed, and even then he took up 'talking' books with enthusiasm) and he read a lot of the books we published, some of them in typescript if the subject interested him. He much admired the work of Alistair Horne and was an active adviser and supporter during the writing of perhaps the best of all his books, *A Savage War of Peace*, the history of the Algerian War, which we published in 1977. Two years later, when Harold finally allowed us to look for a biographer of his own life (the book to be published after his death), he accepted Alistair without hesitation. It took me much longer to persuade Alistair at least to go and talk to the 'subject', but those hours together sealed both their fates and resulted in a two-volume biography of the highest quality and a close friendship for the remaining years of Harold's life. I wish he could have read it, but that was never the plan.

Harold enjoyed the company of writers but he never interfered with the list except 'by invitation'. Our only disaster was quite unexpected, and made a treasured addition to Rebecca's collection of strange and unfortunate happenings.

We had given quite a large party to celebrate Rebecca's 80th birthday and when her 85th was looming up I asked her if she'd like another. She said she felt too old and lame and would I take her out for a quiet lunch? I said yes of course but I thought that Harold would like to be in on it. Would that be all right? 'Yes, indeed it would.' So I asked him and he said he'd take us to Buck's and he'd get his sister-in-law, the Dowager Duchess of Devonshire, to come too. I knew from past happy experience that this would be fine. But on the morning of the lunch he told me that the Duchess had the flu so he'd asked Diana Cooper to come instead. I'd never met her but knew that she and Harold were old and close friends and blithely assumed that as she and Rebecca were both in the business of 'knowing everybody' there would be no problem.

I found out that this was not the case when I picked Rebecca up in a taxi but I still thought that with a bit of luck we'd get by. And so we might have if Harold had not been totally mesmerised by Lady Diana who ignored both of us. Harold said practically nothing to Rebecca and soon gave up altogether, addressing himself exclusively to Lady Diana. By half-time we were reduced to two separate couples, like strangers sharing the same table in a railway buffet. It was an eerie experience, a nightmare version of *Brief Encounter* starring Harold and Diana with Rebecca and me as a pair of intrusive extras. I couldn't see how Rebecca was going to put up with it or why she should even try. But put up with it she did, driven by her insatiable curiosity to know what on earth was going to happen next. Once I realised that she was not going to walk out I began to enjoy myself and we found plenty to talk about, speaking in low enough tones to catch the drift of the rival conversation. I remember saying, 'How will it all end?' and she began to laugh. 'Not well for us, not well.'

The end came quickly enough when Diana peered at her watch and said that she was going to be late for an appointment with her dentist. Harold came gallantly to the rescue and said he would take her in his car. Rebecca thanked him for giving her such a good lunch and as she waved a hand at her opponent she said, to no one in particular, 'Game set and match, I think.' We walked nearly to the end of Savile Row before finding a taxi and she laughed all the way.

Harold and Maurice played Box and Cox with the Chairmanship of Macmillan (depending on whether the Conservatives were in or out of office) until 1974 when Harold, then 80, kicked himself upstairs to become Life President. This didn't stop him from representing the firm on all sorts of exhausting but interesting jaunts, among them, in 1979, a fruitful business trip to China and a dazzlingly successful week launching the *New Grove's Dictionary of Music & Musicians* in New York and Washington. He was fêted wherever he went and he brought style and dash to the role of elder statesman, which kept him in the public eye at home. All this was good for the firm in which he remained the dominant partner. I thought it was hard on Maurice that his father's shadow should grow larger in old age instead of less, but he was remarkably good-humoured about it. 'I'd feel quite naked without it,' he said. But at least he'd had four years in Ted Heath's Cabinet – two of them as Employment Minister, the 'Bed of Nails' for Labour and Conservative alike – and being by nature and conviction a 'Wet' he neither expected nor wanted a seat in the Shadow Cabinet when Mrs Thatcher took over the leadership of their party. More importantly his health deteriorated remorselessly and in 1980 a collapsed lung nearly finished him off. But he battled on for another four years until a new cancer of the lung claimed him.

A month after his father had accepted an earldom as a 90th birthday present from the Queen, I spent an enjoyable day with Maurice at Birch

Grove just before he went into hospital for the last time. He was cheerful enough but doubtful about his chances of surviving another major operation. We talked a lot about Donald and about Dr Dent and he said slyly that if things went wrong at least he would have died sober and notched up another hundred per cent success for Henry and his treatment. I, on the other hand, would still have it to do. I thought we'd been rambling down memory lane for long enough and he was getting tired, so I asked him how he felt about being made a courtesy lord and heir to an earldom. He roused himself and said rather crossly, 'He's held out against it all these years and now he's deprived himself of the distinction of dying plain Mr Macmillan, and what's more he's deprived me of it too. Enough to make one go out and get drunk as a lord.'

I retired at the age of 60 at the end of that year, having spent almost exactly half my life at Macmillan. No regrets – well not many.

Envoi: A Loose End – a ghost story

This sort of highly selective memoir does not lend itself to a satisfactory conclusion because, by its nature, it doesn't have an ending. But those who read the book in typescript said that I couldn't 'just leave it like that' and suggested an Envoi to tie up loose ends and so on. Most of the main characters have a chapter to themselves and all of them are dead. Some rated obituaries in *The Times* and other places where praises are sung, and some of them knew each other. But the only tenuous link between them in this book is that they all played significant parts in my own life at different times. So the Shakespearean device of strewing the stage with corpses is of no use to me and the story (if there is one) is lacking in message, moral or point.

The only character who, true to life, makes brief appearances in many of the chapters is my friend James Farmer. Perhaps he is the joker in my pack, the catcher in my rye and can qualify as a *bona fide* loose end.

Certainly James made me laugh more than anyone I have ever known and the only thing he ever took entirely seriously was his painting. He didn't go in for having friends in high places, was chronically hard-up and needed only food, women and drink to keep him afloat. But he and the writer Frank Tuohy and I had been close friends since we were miserable 13-year-old schoolboys at Stowe and remained inviolably so until James died in 1970 at the age of 45. His death left Frank and me with an unfillable gap in our lives and, between us, the largest collection of his pictures in the world.

There was nothing to laugh at in his final illness. He had been told by a doctor that his liver was in no shape to cope with any further onslaughts of alcohol and that, for him, living was no longer compatible with drinking. After due consideration he decided that he wanted to live, stopped drinking altogether and remained heroically, uncomfortably and, as it turned out, unnecessarily sober for the few months left to him. The diagnosis, although correct, was incomplete and if he had known that he also had lung cancer I suppose that he might have given up smoking as well. It's more likely that he would have opted to keep his familiar comforts to the end. However, he was unaware of the hopelessness of his condition until he went into a London hospital and by then he was too ill to care.

At this time James was living apart from his wife and two children and, for a nominal rent, had been given the run of the top floor of a house in Elsenham Street in Wandsworth by an acquaintance who admired his work. The street name appealed to him because a well-known firm of jam-makers was currently advertising its products as 'Elsenham – the most expensive jam in the world' which neatly summed up his situation.

On the day before the funeral Frank and I went to the house to collect his belongings. These included paintings and drawings which would be needed for the exhibition which the Oxford Gallery had agreed to give him in the autumn. His landlord had been unfailingly kind and helpful to James, thereby incurring the baleful ingratitude with which James often greeted such assistance. Now he helped us to load up the car and it occurred to us that he might like one of the paintings. So Frank asked him and he said that he would like that very much. Unable to leave well alone I added that James would have wanted him to have one.

On the drive back to Kensington where we were to spend the night in the house of one of Frank's cousins, he said crossly, 'Why on earth did you say that? Quite unnecessary and quite untrue.' 'Oh, come on,' I said. 'No harm done and James is hardly in a position to object.'

Frank's cousins were away but had hospitably arranged for their cook Leah, a very small black girl from the Seychelles, to give us supper. It had been a long, cold, glum day and the prospect of hot soup and casserole was very welcome. The house was warm and I took off my jacket, hung it over the back of my chair and put my cigarettes and a box of Swan Vestas in my trouser pocket. Leah was charming and giggly as she placed bowls of steaming soup in front of us. I was just about to pull my chair closer to the table when, for the second time in my life, I experienced an agonising, burning sensation in my trousers. The first time had been 27 years earlier when I was a Private in the Army and a box of Swan Vestas had exploded in the trouser pocket of my battledress. So I knew what had happened and what to do.

I sprang to my feet with a yelp of pain and alarm and tore off my trousers. Leah, fearing the worst, screamed and made a despairing dash for the door, but fell over before she reached it. Frank sat like a stunned ox. It all happened within the space of a few seconds.

But there was no smoke and no fire. My thighs were covered in hot tomato soup and several feet away the empty bowl sat demurely on the table.

Leah had stopped screaming, and was cowering wide-eyed against the door. Frank and I stared at each other and slowly began to laugh – great aching sobs of laughter. When he could speak he said, 'I *knew* you shouldn't have said that. I *told* you so!'

I'd brought a funeral-going suit with me and, while I was changing into another pair of trousers, Frank apologised to Leah for my clumsiness with the soup bowl and for giving her such a fright. I was not an impulsive rapist. It seemed better not to tell her that she had just witnessed an interesting and hilarious rebuke from beyond the grave.

We decided to have another go at supper, leaving out the soup this time. I ate warily but James had made his point and the casserole was excellent.

I don't think there is exactly a moral to this story, but it does suggest that there can be no loose endings for a loose cannon.

Appendix
Apomorphine in the Treatment of Addiction and Anxiety

by John Yerbury Dent, LMSSA,
Visiting Physician, Spelthorne St Mary, Thorpe

(Reprinted from *The Medical Press*, May 1961)

As long ago as 1899 Dr Douglas, an American, noticed improvement after an injection of apomorphine in an alcoholic who was suffering from delirium. I can find no record of Douglas treating another case but in about 1910 Hare in England used apomorphine to remove alcohol from his patients and to calm them and he wrote enthusiastically about its effects. Again no-one seems to have followed up his work. In 1922 I used it to remove alcohol from those who had taken sufficient to make them very drunk or comatose and then give it to alcoholics who were not drunk but who were given a drink after each injection. I gave three or four injections followed by some spirit daily for two or three days.

The Aversion Fallacy

Quite independently the Russians began doing this at about the same time, producing a Pavlovian conditioned aversion. The aversion does not last very long, in some cases only a few days, and aversion itself is not sufficient to stop a compulsive drinker from taking the alcohol he needs. This aversion treatment was improved by Voegtlin and Lemere in Seattle by the substitution of emetine for apomorphine. Emetine produces a much greater aversion, a much more violent sickness and one that continues longer. It does not tend to put the patient to sleep, as apomorphine does, so his discomfort is greater and he is fully conscious of it. To increase the discomfort they sometimes gave amphetamine by mouth between the vomits and in the early days some who used this method poured the vomit back into the patient. This was aversion *in excelsis.*

I found that the patients who did not vomit all their alcohol did not do as well as those who did; so, in order to produce the vomit in those who were not sick, I tickled their throats with a feather to get up the alcohol. Then I found that aversion was only a small and unimportant factor in the curative process because I had a few cases who had no sense of smell or taste and therefore no aversion was developed, yet they did as well as the others.

It was quickly noticeable that, however successful the treatment, very small quantities of alcohol would bring back the need for it no matter how long the patient had been free from any craving. I have known one glass of sherry do this in a man who had been happily teetotal for eleven years, during which time he had served all kinds of drinks in the bar of the hotel he owned. He drank half a bottle of whisky that night and a whole bottle the next day and had to be treated again. Thus it seemed that the apomorphine produced some change in the mechanism of the patient which a small amount of alcohol would reverse.

I found that apomorphine was very quickly destroyed in the body; for large quantities can be given every half-hour and it does not seem to accumulate. This made me alter my treatment because, if I stopped giving apomorphine at the same time I stopped giving alcohol, a few hours later, if all the alcohol had not been promptly vomited, there would still be alcohol in the patient and not apomorphine, and it would be as if he had taken another drink.

From then onwards I gave apomorphine, as previously, two hourly until the blood pressure dropped; but I continued to give apomorphine in just sub-vomiting doses three hourly for the next 48 hours, during which time the patient was eating and drinking as much soft drink as he liked, and the results of my treatment were very much better. I did not mind whether the patient vomited or not during the first part of the treatment. I did not mind whether he got aversion or not; I did not mind if he vomited his tea or other soft drinks in the second part of the treatment. Even if he did vomit, he did not develop any aversion to the soft drink. A big factor in the treatment must have been the removal or reversal of the craving for alcohol.

In my first paper, 25 years ago, I unfortunately thought and said that apomorphine treatment was a purely aversive one. It does produce aversion in most cases of alcohol addiction, but it is just as efficient in the treatment of addiction to morphine and its derivatives and to pethidine and it is only a little less efficient in the treatment of barbiturate and paraldehyde addiction as these latter require at least 14 days treatment.

Method of Treatment of Alcoholics

When a patient comes to me I am not interested in what started him on his addiction. I give him apomorphine gr. 1/40 intramuscularly and 1–2 ounces of whisky or gin mixed with the same quantity of water. This dose seldom makes him vomit but generally makes him a little sleepy. If he is not sick I increase the dose a little two hours later and then for about 48 hours he has just nauseating injections two hourly during the day and, at night, not less frequently than three hourly if he sleeps but two hourly if he is awake. He has no other drink or food but he can have as much as he likes of the whisky or gin and water, a glass of which is always within his reach. His urine is tested with Benedict's solution for sugar and the test shows about ¼ per cent of a reducing substance within the first 24 hours; then, curiously enough, it shows less or even no reduction at all, and the test increases again up to about ¼ per cent: when this occurs I take him off the alcohol, for which he is very grateful, and he is given soft drinks containing quantities of glucose and a little salt. This sugar test is a better method than my earlier one of waiting for the blood pressure to fall, as the urine change takes place after two days whereas the blood pressure took almost three days to fall and the patient was left in an unnecessarily weak condition. All patients are, of course, given large doses of the B vitamins by mouth.

The acetone in the patient's urine shows a continuous rise during the first 48 hours of the treatment. During this early stage he is passing a form of sugar while he is being given none; during the late stages he is given a lot of sugar and at first he passes a lot, but by the end of the week, though he is still taking a lot, he is passing none. He is using up sugar far more efficiently than he was at the beginning of the treatment. His taste for sweets develops. The typical alcoholic does not like sweet drinks. He apparently needs his alcohol partly because he is not able to get all the nourishment he requires from glucose.

Later Development of the Treatment

I was lucky enough to have a patient who came to be treated for alcoholism and, on his leaving home, his private nurse who called for him said, 'I suppose I must go on with the injections?' She had been giving him morphine two or three times a day on the advice of his doctor in an attempt to cut down his drinking. I had not previously been told about this. He had been given up to a grain and a half a day for months. Apomorphine not only removed his need for drink, it removed his need for morphine, as well. Then I successfully treated morphine, methadone, heroin, pethidine, paraldehyde and barbiturate addicts with alcohol and apomorphine, exactly as if they were alcoholics. (Incidentally all these drugs are sugar sparers.) In these cases conditioned aversion to the drug is quite impossible and can take no part at all in the satisfactory result. They have taken their drug subcutaneously or intravenously and they are given little or no drug during the treatment, so we must look for some other cause for this improvement in their condition by apomorphine than an aversion to their drug of addiction.

Treatment of Drug Addiction

When a drug addict comes to me he generally expects his treatment to take several months. He expects the dose to be cut down gradually and the longer this takes the better he would be pleased. When I tell him he will not be hospitalized for more than a fortnight he gets scared but I also tell him that I will give him the drug he needs whenever he asks for it and in the dose he demands, if he will promise not to ask unless he is really needing it.

I tell him that he will be given apomorphine followed by a short drink of gin or whisky and water every two hours. The name apomorphine pleases him, but I have known two morphine-addicted doctors object to the idea of taking spirits. They both said 'I have taken drugs for years but I have never sunk to an addiction to alcohol.' I then tell them that alcohol will increase the action of the apomorphine and they will not have to take it more than a few days, and that I do not intend to change them from morphinism to alcoholism.

I then treat them in the same way as if they were alcoholics except that I give them water and liquid foods as well as doses of the necessary vitamins. During the whole of the treatment they are not given their drugs of addiction unless they ask for them and they are extremely surprised how little they need. They are on their honour to ask for as little as possible and I have known some who never asked for any, their deprivation symptoms being so slight. Some get hallucinations and even delirium, but these are lessened by promazine, 100 mg. intramuscularly 6 or 8 hourly, and minute doses of morphine, gr. 1/16, or its equivalent of their other drug. The apomorphine is continued sometimes as frequently as ½ hourly in doses of about half what had been their vomiting dose earlier in the treatment.

If they do not have delirium or when they are sane again after having it, they sometimes, generally four days after the last dose of their drug, ask for more drug, just a very little, and I say that they can have it but they must have a little spirit first; this they generally refuse because they have developed an aversion to alcohol and I use this aversion test to give me a measure of their need for the drug. If a real craving had developed, no nauseous taste would prevent them from taking it. This is a very valuable test and is one of the reasons for giving alcohol to these addicts. The patient also knows that he will receive sub-nauseating injections of apomorphine 3 hourly for 48 hours after his last dose of alcohol.

I never give anything for sleeplessness except small doses of apomorphine by injection or sublingually. Sleep may be absent for 3 or 4 days or more, but the time goes more quickly if the nurses are tactful and cheerful and give frequent little meals and keep them from trying to go to sleep. It is better to encourage them to talk and to try to keep awake, for trying is always failing: nearly everyone can sleep when it is time to get up.

Paraldehyde addiction is the worst to treat, for its heavy molecule takes a long time to get out of the body: so I keep paraldehyde patients as quiet as possible by injections of apomorphine for a whole week before starting on the serious business of treatment. All cured drug addicts should be teetotallers after treatment as they will rapidly switch from alcohol on to stronger and stronger drugs.

I have treated a doctor who was taking 4,000 mg. of pethidine daily by injection and 17 full doses (51 grains) of Nembutal nightly and was still not able to sleep. He was in my care for eleven days and the only sedative he received besides one bottle of gin was 1,400 mp. of pethidine on the first day, 800 on the second and 250 on the third. He has been happily carrying on a heavy practice for the past ten months without any drug or alcohol at all and has put on a very welcome one and a half stones in weight.

Addiction to drugs is often traced to some sudden trouble or family tragedy for which the drug was prescribed. What should have been given was a sharp dose of apomorphine. Sedative drugs should never be given for sleep and if given for pain they should never relieve the whole of the pain but only make it bearable and be refused as early as possible during recovery.

A Senseless Fear of Apomorphine

In North America both in the States and in Canada, there is a perfectly senseless refusal to treat addictions with apomorphine. When recently I asked an eminent American pharmacologist the reason for this, he said 'We have enough addictions on our hands we do not want to add to them an addiction to apomorphine.' Addiction to apomorphine is quite impossible because if it is taken for any length of time the taker develops a negative tolerance, smaller and smaller quantities produce vomiting. Apomorphine is not used in the Federal hospitals for drug addicts in the States. Methadone (Physeptone) is given to replace heroin or morphine, being intermediate in its strength but found, it is said, to produce milder withdrawal symptoms though they may last longer than either.

Apomorphine is not even in the dispensaries of many of our mental hospitals. One doesn't run a garage without a spanner. In treating sudden mania and many other psychotic conditions apomorphine should at least be tried. At one of the leading psychological hospitals in Britain some years ago I did persuade one of the principal psychiatrists to give apomorphine. He did take the dreadful risk of doing so: he gave gr. 1/20 to two patients, but the nurses objected because these patients were sick, so no more was given. This was about 20 years ago and apparently the nurses are still dictating the treatment at that hospital.

Unfortunately, about the beginning of the century, it was used in some mental hospitals and homes as a punishment for obstreporous inmates: 'If you do not behave yourself I'll give you a shot.' Patients were often quieter 'after a shot,' not because they were frightened of getting another but because their mental disturbance was relieved. It is a tragedy that what was possibly the very best treatment was given, not as a treatment but as a punishment, and that it was therefore quickly and rightly suppressed. Doctors are not punishers but healers and apomorphine got a bad reputation; because the intention was wrong, the good effect of apomorphine on a multitude of sufferers has been postponed for 60 years.

Fleming saw penicillin destroying his beautiful pet cultures for ten years; it was a criminal and must not be allowed entrance to the hospital. Fortunately he could not keep it out.

The treatment of addiction or anxiety states by apomorphine is not taught in our medical schools and has yet to appear in medical textbooks. The Society for the Study of Addiction is now 75 years old and has only about 200 medical members scattered over the world and less than ten medical men in Britain in charge of mental hospitals or of avowed homes for alcoholics are members of this, the only society anywhere whose interest is in addiction per se and the multitude of ills that burgeon from it.

Essentially addiction is a medical disease with psychological overtones. It is useless to attempt psychotherapy before the addiction and craving has been removed, but one or two doses of waking suggestion, by which I mean encouraging talks to the patient while he is reading aloud rather quickly about half a column of a newspaper, to readjust his unconscious habits to fit more comfortably with his conscious desires, are very helpful and are all that is necessary. It is, of course, a form of hypnosis which anyone can give to anyone who is sane enough to pay full attention to his reading. I often teach married couples to give this help to each other.

If any institutions in Britain would like it, I am prepared to give them all the assistance I can in showing them how, or helping them, to give apomorphine to their patients. It is a practical treatment which is admittedly difficult to learn from the printed page. The biggest difficulty is to teach nurses to make a satisfactory job of what is pre-eminently an expert nursing treatment, requiring tact and understanding as well as devoted and strictly efficient observance of the important details of their duty.

Dr J. A. Hobson, who has used apomorphine in cases of addiction for many years at the Middlesex Hospital, rightly said at a lecture he gave at the Royal Society of Medicine, 'Addiction is the only disease in which the worse the condition the better the prognosis.'

Every doctor who begins to use apomorphine for addiction or anxiety states will rapidly become intensely interested in this remarkable drug and have many very grateful patients and their friends.

Index